Beyond THE WALL

20 UNTOLD IMMIGRANT STORIES:
FROM SURVIVAL TO SUCCESS

ESMERALDA CASTELAN
GUADALUPE TOVAR

Beyond THE WALL

This book is a compilation of stories from numerous people who have each contributed a chapter and is designed to provide inspiration to our readers.

Printed in the United States of America

BEYONDTHEWALLBOOKS.COM

ISBN: 978-0-9990012-7-1

"American food is immigrant food, and it all has a story on how it became a part of the fabric of American culture. Pizza and bagels weren't always considered American food, but now they are staples in homes across the country. The traditional dishes brought to us by Latino immigrants have stories to be told and flavors to be shared. Beyond the Wall captures this by highlighting the experiences and favorite recipes of Latino immigrant culinary greats, including Miguel Gonzalez, who owns and operates Los Comales Restaurants in my beloved hometown, Chicago. Buen Provecho!"

– Rep. Luis V. Gutierrez (D-IL-04)

"Con el estilo particular de una narrativa sobre la migración de latinoamericanos a los Estados Unidos, y una combinación compartida desde la experiencia personal, Esmeralda Castelán y Guadalupe Tovar han hecho de esta experiencia una exposición de la migración que podemos entender desde dos puntos de vista totalmente antropológicos, es decir, el cómo integrarse positivamente en una sociedad desconocida, y el otro, cómo dejar atrás a la dependencia social que se abandona, si en ella está todo lo que te identifica: la familia, los amigos, las costumbres y tradiciones, la gastronomía, y porqué no, todo aquello que motivó a un ser humano, a dejar atrás su historia y origen. Aplaudo el esfuerzo que se realizó, tanto de quién buscó y seleccionó las historias, como de quién las escribió; conjuntar apoyos para lograr un gran libro de experiencias con la visión del éxito, logros de vida para "sobrevivir" y que día a día siguen dando una pauta ejemplar para quiénes son migrantes y para quiénes piensan iniciar una travesía y lo serán. Una lectura totalmente recomendable para entender "casi" en primera persona la experiencia de ser migrante."

– Ana Laura Martinez de Lara,
Director of Instituto Nacional Electoral, Mexico

"Esmeralda and Guadalupe present us with a very timely book in *Beyond the Wall*. The best way to counteract false narratives about our community is with the truth. This mother daughter duo not only presents the reader food for thought in these immigrant success stories, but literally offers savory recipes from those profiled in the book! You can't beat that! Enjoy!"

– Martin R. Castro, CEO, Castro Synergies, LLC.

"If you want to be inspired or to remember enjoying a simple pleasure of life tasting food that someday made us happy, *Beyond the wall* is an engaging little book full of life stories to read. The stories of chefs depict the growth of their wisdom in the face of adversity and together conform a harvest of redemptive insights that will both motivate you and make you eager to want to enjoy the food they cook as you get to know more about them."

– Ramiro J. Atristain-Carrion, Financial advisor, Professor, Life Coach, author of photobooks and cooking aficionado.

This book is a kaleidoscope of styles, a mosaic of different life stories seasoned with cooking recipes. Although they are different life experiences, these stories have a constant thread: they are epics of people who have risen from poverty, from material constraints and, at times, affective, to reaching unsuspected heights of realization in their respective fields of human activity. This work is an ode to migrants and the culture that characterizes them: the culture of effort, of sacrifice, of generosity. In times of adversity and challenges for migrants in the United States, this book comes to vindicate the work and contribution that these people is making to the greatness of this country.

– Carlos Valera Paulino, Community Affairs Consul of Mexico in Chicago

"*Beyond the Wall* will make you feel everything is possible through determination and hard work. Guadalupe and Esmeralda tell us the stories of immigrants whose love and passion for gastronomy have changed, for good, the lives of those around them; but above all, it is the story of those who started a journey far from their land to become a better version of themselves. With no doubts, this is an inspiring book that arrives in a moment when, more than ever, it is necessary to acknowledge our immigrants and their contribution to this country."

– Carlos Jiménez Macías, Consul General of Mexico in Chicago

"The flavors and colors of our gastronomy are a crucial and important part of our culture. The smells of corianden and "sofrito" always mentally and emotionally transport us to better times, to sweet anoances of our lands and it does not matter where we are, they remind us of who we are and the value of our culture. *Beyond the Wall* is a book that more than share recipes and culinary tricks, shares the passion, determination and success of extraordinary human beings who fought for their dreams and became an example of our community. I invite you to discover in these pages, the richness of our culture, the delight of our food and the unwavering desire to succed of Latinos in the United States."

– Deyanira Martinez, Journalist/ Author/TV Personality and Diversity and Inclusion advocate

---

"Beyond the Wall is a book to be read and to remind us of the values that make our traditions. The combination of motivational stories with heart-warming recipes makes this book a must read."

– Dr. Javier Laguna, Director of a Prestigious Mexican University in Chicago

"In this exquisite, delicious and tasty read, each story contains passion, courage, love and hope that each immigrant brings with them and that forces us to do our best in the name of Latinos and Latinas. In *Beyond the Wall*, Esmeralda and Lupe narrate masterfully why the culinary art of Latinos is the essence of every restaurant and a tool of progress in the cities of the USA today. As an immigrant or immigrant supporter, you cannot miss this recipe to getting the American dream."

– Javier Salas -Talk Radio Host

"¡Muchas Gracias Guadalupe y Esmeralda! Thank you for taking us in a delicious journey of lives seasoned with love, passion, faith, courage, curiosity, discipline, perseverance, hard work ethic and many more ingredients that make our culture so enjoyable and admirable. These encouraging stories of restauranteurs that have gone from less to success, made me hungry for more... more of the qualities that make someone overcome the most difficult situations while taking pride of their humble beginnings. I accept the challenge to place each of these culinary embassies in my bucket list. From champions like these; I expect more than a culinary experience. I am looking forward to life lessons to become a blessing, and not a burden, beyond the wall."

– Pastor Lopez, Calvary Church

"*Beyond the Wall* is a book that tells the stories of fearless people who one day decided to leave their land to build new lives, reinventing themselves in a foreign soil. It is also a particular collection of stories with much more to read between lines. The duo mother and daughter as authors will introduce the reader to the world of feelings and adventures of those, who feed America everyday with dishes prepared with dreams and hopes as their main ingredients, stories that only can be told from a female perspective."

– Esther Quintero Guzman M.Sc, Associate Director of Regional Initiatives in the Office of Global Engagement at a Major University

Dedication:

THIS BOOK IS DEDICATED TO ALL THE
DREAMERS. THOSE WHO STARTED THE
MARCH TOWARDS A BETTER FUTURE, THOSE
WHO WERE LOOKING FOR A SECOND CHANCE
OR MAYBE A NEW BEGINNING. TO THOSE
WHOSE LAST GOODBYES WERE A BURNING
DESERT FLOOR AND THE SCENT OF HOME
CARRIED AWAY IN A GUST OF WIND, WHOSE
EFFORTS WERE NOT ANY LESS, FOR IT
CARRIED THEM TO THE GLORY. TO THE ONES
WHO CONTINUE TO DREAM OF A MOTHER
OR FATHERS HUG ACCOMPANIED BY THE
LAUGHTER OF A LOVED ONE. BUT ABOVE ALL,
THIS IS FOR THOSE WHEREVER YOU MAY BE,
WHO LIVE DREAMING OF TAKING A STEP JUST
BEYOND THE WALL.

ACKNOWLEDGMENTS

I want to thank God first and foremost for granting me the ability to complete this project.

To my husband David Castelán, for being the head of this family, your daily struggle, the unwavering love for your family, and above all for supporting and financing this project. Thank you Jacqueline Camacho, for depositing your experience and confidence into making this book, and believing in our vision. Not to mention, the constant support from the JJR agency that made this all possible. To Irene Anzola, who always had the right words and motivation to carry out this project and push it ahead. Day in and day out I saw the sacrifices you made for this project as if it were your own, believe me when I say your efforts never went unappreciated. Lastly, to you my little girl, Esmeralda, since you first opened your eyes you performed the greatest act of love. Thank you for your immense talent and long nights invested into this book.

– Guadalupe Tovar

HOW TO USE THIS BOOK

The Beyond the Wall book is composed of 2 parts and a total of 23 riveting life stories. The first half of stories consists of 20 latino immigrants whom have dedicated their lives work to the culinary world. Blossoming from the unbreakable vision of mother, Guadalupe Tovar, Esmeralda Castelan beautifully retells these stories with her poetic writing style and metaphoric rhetoric in order to not only tug at the readers heart strings, but transport them to horizons never before encountered.

The last 3 showcase the journey of various latino community leaders. People who have focused their time and energy into bettering the community and helping individuals find their own path of success.

Beyond the Wall attempts to expose the undeniable values and principles engraved within latino culture, and the typical sayings that made them impossible to forget. Along with this comes the various traditions and latino dishes that have served to not only feed stomachs, but add a special spice to life. It's the dishes of our mothers, aunts, and fathers who reek of struggle and persistence, yet never fail to provoke a nostalgic smile. This book was formed to share the true colors of latino hearts and with the idea that hope is always waiting beyond the wall.

TABLE OF CONTENTS

PART ONE
The Immigrant Stories

PART TWO
Community Leaders

PART ONE

THE IMMIGRANT STORIES

CHEF CARLOS GAYTÁN

Mexique Restaurant

—

1

Perseverance

I come from a very small town in Guerrero, Mexico where—as a child and as an adolescent—there were only two very apparent options: either you were the type to become an alcoholic or your mind was always in the game spending endless hours playing sports in less than adequate terrain.

So, you can see that I didn't exactly come from a movie star city where everyone was bound to become something great. I came from a home that didn't necessarily scream fortune but held more value than any lavish mansion. One could say that hard work was not even taught at the time. It was just a quality that was naturally picked up or blossomed in due time much like the entrance of puberty.

I can remember my day-to-day routine of going out to fetch the day's meal in a supermarket that was unlike the ones most people are accustomed to, mine didn't have sweet greeters that welcomed you upon entrance. There was no international section or wide variety display with strategically shelved produce to lure people in. There wasn't much in my market, but from what there was, it was all good. It came in abundance, it came with no limitations, and best of all it was given to me for free by Mother Nature herself, a little place we called the forest.

There, in the wild, was my little market. This is where I grew to know food—not just as a vital way of sustaining life, but more as a seasoning to it.

We did not come from much, so therefore it made it difficult for us to obtain much. From an adopted form of survival, my mother found ways of pushing us along, and mealtime was no different. If we didn't have one thing it was never a problem because my mom would find a substitute, and I would bring it to her from the forest. One can say that it was a primal way of living, but I loved it. I loved feeling the earth beneath my feet as I scrounged up herbs and berries. I loved knowing that I was contributing to our household. But, most of all, I loved seeing what type of concoctions my mother would create. It was her creativity in the kitchen that taught me to never put limits on anything.

Now, what do I mean by that? What could my mom possibly make that could stir up such emotion in a man? Well of course I grew up eating lovely and typical Mexican dishes, but they were anything but traditional. See, my mom didn't fit into that category because we didn't use typical ingredients. We had the foundations of the dish, and the rest—any missing piece—we could find in the forest. She did whatever she could to give us this.

At the age of 21, I decided to move to the U.S. leaving my family and forest behind, not really having a plan but knowing that whatever it was I was looking for would be there. I got near to Chicago, visited family members, then headed straight for the Windy City.

My first job was at a Sheraton North Hotel where I started off with humble beginnings. I knew that I didn't want to just stay in that position, and that I not only had the capabilities, but also the interest to do so much more. I started noticing everything in the kitchen: the little things, how foods were handled, where things went, the movements of each chef at work. At that time, I only worked in the afternoons until I realized that wasn't enough for what I wanted to accomplish. I wasn't able to feed my hunger to learn and create.

The next week, I went up to my boss and asked if I could go in and work the morning shift as well. I figured there must be something else, something more that I wasn't getting in the afternoon that maybe with just more time I'd be able to grasp. To push the offer even farther, I told him candidly that I just wanted to learn, and I wanted to do it here at his restaurant. I told him there was no need to pay me for the extra time as long he let me work. Luckily, he quickly agreed, and my life shortly became centered around the kitchen.

Once I started working mornings, I had the honor of meeting Chef Michael Garbin who became my mentor in the kitchen. I, a young 21-year-old who had never worked in a formal kitchen who wasn't accustomed to typical "anything" and who didn't even speak the language of the country in which he now called home, was being taught by a man like Chef Garbin. Right there was when I began to see all the possibilities life really had to offer. Don't get confused with the dreamy scent of opportunity. I was still nowhere near ready to become a chef, let alone the man I am today. I started at the very bottom of the "totem pole" in terms of kitchen duties. I held basically every position that kitchen had to offer, did the jobs no one in their right minds wanted to do, and secretly archived the skills of those higher in rank that surrounded me.

The odd thing is none of this ever felt like extra work to me. How could it? Waking up to a kitchen every morning produced the purest form of happiness because I knew that this is where my dreams stemmed from, that this is where I would make nothing into everything. As my day progressed, with Chef Garbin as my mentor, I remember feeling excitement, a simple joy rush through me at seeing the flutter of chefs preparing meals. The chaos in the kitchen didn't seem like chaos but a strategic dance. I remember knowing I wanted to be a part of that dance, better yet, I needed to be the ringleader. I obviously took my job very seriously—so much so that Chef Garbin began taking me with him to private events and banquets as part of the cooking staff there.

Everything seemed to be panning out better than I could have ever hoped for in a million years, but I'd be lying if I said my life was picture perfect. See, even though God was bringing various blessings into my new life, they also came with the unexpected pain a young twenty-something-year-old kid wasn't so focused on.

Sometimes it's so easy to get caught up in working and learning and the execution of this illustrious pioneer plan that one doesn't even notice that day by day you're slowly falling apart. The first two years that I arrived in the U.S. were among the hardest even with the amazing steps I was taking in the workplace. No amount of success compares to coming "home" to an empty building you call "home" that you pay as your "home," but lacks everything that is *home*. I only really had one cousin here with me, but he of course was busy with his own life and maintaining his own business. So, in a sense, yes, I was alone. Yes, I was lonely.

I think you get to this moment of shock when it finally hits you, and you might as well be living on a different planet because the emotion is the same. It's that feeling of solitude and loss that welcomes itself late at night as you picture your mother placing your neatly folded clothes on top of your bed as you are thrusting them into a plastic hamper in the back of a twenty-four-hour laundromat. It's not having her morning list of chores making you contemplate even moving out of bed while smelling Grandma's delicious frijoles oozing through the walls forcing you to put one foot in front of the other. It's looking at the sky, moon, and sun knowing they've always been the same, but somehow feeling distant from them as if they've now become strangers because even they had a distinct glow that didn't transfer across borders. The worst part of it all was when my body would decide to shut down and the back of my mother's hand was nowhere to be found and nowhere near the warm skin of my forehead determining whether I had a fever or not. Moments like these and actions like these may not seem extravagant, but it hurts to know that there is no one out there looking out for you to tell you to put a coat on or to take this medicine or drink this remedy. Moments like these leave you so alone in a busy world.

Though these feelings were always present, I had to force myself to get up and keep going, and with time, it got easier as I kept investing myself into my job. I soon got the chance to cook for a private, high-class establishment, the Union League Club. Although it was a place where I really enjoyed cooking, I continued working hand-in-hand with Chef Garbin, constantly trying to better myself and prove to him what I was capable of.

Time went by, and the kind of events I was cooking for kept growing, but there is one in particular that I believe was the turning point in my career.

My boss at the time, who was also the executive chef of our team, was contacted by the French embassy to cater for a massive event of 600 or 700 people. In short, he accepted, the date was set and all that was left to do was wait for it to actually happen.

Of course, anytime you get a big client like the French Ambassador, it's exciting, but—not to toot my horn—I had been cooking for many people for a long time, and I knew my way around this particular kitchen, so I wouldn't say I was more nervous than usual.

The day of the event arrived and my task force—which only consisted of about seven or eight people, half of whom are on dish duty—are at the Union League Club setting up and getting ready. As we got there, a man walked up to me and introduced himself as the French chef who came along on behalf of the embassy. Our greeting was pleasant, but the next chunk of our conversation was anything but that. With a strong look, he asked how I was and if I was ready for the night. I gave him a reassuring smile and replied, "Super ready." We talked for a bit, and then he proceeded to ask where Chef Garbin was. I responded a little hesitantly saying that I didn't know, but that he usually leaves around 5 so that was probably a better indication of his whereabouts. Well, let's just say Mr. French Chef was not too happy about having the executive chef of my team missing the night of his country's embassy dinner.

"What?! What do you mean he's not here? Doesn't he know how important this night is for me?"

Not to try and degrade his worry because I understood his desire for a successful dinner, but I knew who my team was and what we were capable of creating. I mean for Christ sakes, I had been leading these cooks through many meals with the chef, and I was the one who was coordinating and creating dishes for our menus. Me, the kid who used to go shopping for produce in his backyard was now having other people come to him for help on their food. In that moment, I knew I had to prove myself not only to this man, but to everyone, that I could handle the pressure. My mantra of always serving the best was not going to die that night. After all, that's what I lived for: to serve.

I promised the chef that there was no need for worry and assured him my team and I were going to serve the best dinner, and the night was going to turn out great. Obviously, he didn't agree right away, but after some pushes and shoves—metaphorically speaking—we made an agreement in which if, at any time, it was evident that we couldn't handle it, he could jump in and take over.

Well, guess what? I made a promise and came through. Not once did the chef had to step in. If anything, I think he might have been more astonished at the work we did and the flawless night we were able to execute with such short means. The most surprising event of the night for me was having the French chef come up to me with such humility and courage and say, "I'm sorry for doubting you and your team; it was an excellent job you all did today. I can honestly say I've never met someone like you in the kitchen."

Not long after, maybe about two weeks or so passed by, when I got a call from the French embassy offering me a position as an executive chef at a highly renowned French restaurant here in Chicago. As amazing as the opportunity appeared, I was honest with him and above all else honest with myself that I didn't know anything about cooking French food or even the roots and principles of cooking French cuisine. I humbly told the man on the phone this and asked if he was then willing to teach me. So, for the next four months that was my new task: to tackle the art of French cuisine.

Looking back on it now, one of the main things I've noticed is that I didn't go looking for all of these things that happened to me. Yes, I put myself in a basic situation of where I wanted to be, but everything else—all the extra jobs and contacts—those found me. When I started working for the French restaurant, I didn't go in demanding so and so pay. They willingly offered one that was well above my original pay grade, and I was immensely thankful for it.

So, I continued at the French restaurant until that business ended. Up to that point, it seemed as if many things in my life did not go according to my original plan, but that was so much better. I saw the closing of the restaurant as a window to try something that had been on my heart for some time, a subject that had occupied so many restless nights and discussions with my wife: I wanted to open my own restaurant.

I deliberated for some time and mentioned the idea to my wife asking her opinion on the opportunity, and I'll never forget what she responded to me. It was a short and maybe anticlimactic response, but it was just what I needed to get the wheels rolling on my next project. When I told her about the restaurant, she simply smiled at me and said, "Go for it."

That was the beginning of Mexique.

From my story thus far, it's easy to assume that I've done it all and that a restaurant was the perfect next step, but as plans began to unfold, I realized I had no experience in working at a real Mexican restaurant. Typical Mexican restaurants weren't exactly loving the food I was making either because it wasn't the traditional way.

You don't follow step-by-step ingredients in a restaurant and make food the way I grew up loving food.

I did, though, eventually get a job, but the only problem was no one wanted me as a chef. So, I was pushed towards managerial roles that I hated because I always felt as if I was the police of the kitchen. I no longer felt that passion and love that I had grown so accustomed to. In fact, I felt uncomfortable in a kind of environment I was so used to calling home. The only good thing that really came from that was the day I was let go. Word got around that I was planning to open my own restaurant, and stemming from a feeling of threat and fear, I was let go under the impression that I would steal the restaurant's recipes and sell them as my own.

At the moment, the severity of the situation didn't really hit me. I figured I already had the location for my business. We bought the building. Our plans had started, but then reality hit hard like a boulder. I was sitting in my living room with my family, and I was unemployed. My wife who had been among the biggest pillars in all of this—who quit her job as an architect to help me out—was also unemployed, and we had a million things to still prepare and pay. It was a tough moment for me, and I began to doubt all of my plans because they no longer just consisted of me; I now had a family, children to support and people watching me. And as hard as the situation seemed, it served as a way to push me out of the darkness. So, I just looked at my wife and said, "Honey, you know we're already half way there, and I don't think we can or should stop. Let's just go full force like there is no turning back."

So we did. Not much later, our restaurant was built and "Mexique" was born.

If this was a perfect fairy tale, after my rough patch, things would get better, the restaurant would open, the whole town would fall in love, and we'd all live happily ever . . . but that didn't happen.

As you can imagine, no one knew "Carlos Gaytan" and because of that no one wanted to put a dollar—a penny towards me. Plus, it didn't help that we opened right when the economy started crashing. I wasn't quite sure about what to do. I couldn't believe that everything I had invested in could so quickly turn into nothing. I was lost, and I reached out to a person and explained the situation, to which he just pushed and urged me to seek God even more during this troubling time. He asked if I had sought for help from investors who knew more about this, and I, of course, had already done it, but no one was interested in an entrepreneur with no solid credentials.

Before our call ended and noticing my distress, the gentleman left me with this, "Carlos, I'm going to give you one piece of advice, and I want you to please follow it. Tonight I want you to just get on your knees, gather your family, and pray." I'll be the first one to admit that during my time here, I wasn't really too concerned with my relationship with God. Honestly, I wasn't even sure we even had one, but the worst of times brings out the most unexpected of believers, and I needed a miracle. I remember having bills piled up not knowing where I was going to pull from in order to pay them off and still be smiling at my kids telling them my day was great because maybe—just maybe—if I said it enough it would become true. You end up lying so much to yourself and avoiding the facts because it doesn't seem fair for something that meant so much, something that took all your heart could quickly be deemed nothing and so quickly be taken away.

I would look at my restaurant and see "Carlos Gaytan." I saw myself running home to the smell of my mom's moles, to her enchiladas. I could feel the hearth of my grandma's laughter as I inhaled her famous frijoles knowing that food like that was priceless—something I would never find anywhere else, that I would never be able to recreate, nor did I want to because that was God's gift bestowed to my mother. I looked around the restaurant that I constructed, the floors that I placed, the decorative pieces my wife picked. I saw everything that this place was supposed to be and as quickly as those thoughts came they vanished. Miracles do happen, and prayer is a powerful thing because the next day I got a call from the bank asking if I was Carlos Gaytan to which I responded "Yes," and to this day, I wonder if whomever I was talking to on the phone that day knows what they did for me. It seemed as if every sound around me dissipated into nothing.

"Carlos, we've been looking into some things and the bank actually has some money that it wants to give to you and your business." The amount was the exact amount that I needed in order to fully finish my project.

We got through that one struggle and continued on, and the business got a bit better, but it wasn't anything that was changing my life in the long run. And then the economy hit us hard. We seemed to have gotten out of so many struggles before, but there didn't seem to be a way out of this one.

The only option I could see was selling the restaurant because there was just no revenue coming in. I couldn't help but break down in tears facing what I was trying to believe was all a bad dream, but I now knew selling might just have to be my next step. I went to my wife and asked if we could pray together because I had reached a point where there was no earthly thing that could help me. I didn't quite know how to start or what to say. I was sitting there hopeless in tears talking to a man, a God, I didn't even know. I asked Him if He remembered me. I begged him to please remember me. Here is what I whispered: *I was once, not too long ago, a young kid who just wanted to serve people to help them. I was the one that you helped so many times, and who sees now that your hand was behind everything I ever did. Please help me now.*

I told my wife that I thought we should sell the restaurant. I was expecting her to give me a definite answer of what I should do, but she left it up to me, telling me that if I thought it was the thing to do then I should do it. Again, I was in the same place I had been so many times just looking for a way out, when I was saved by a call again. I had a man call to congratulate me because I was mentioned in *Brahman* magazine, a great honor in the restaurant world. I thanked him but was confused as to why he was calling me. He began telling me how his company had been following me for a long time, and he was very proud to let me know that I had earned a Michelin star. For those of you who don't know what a Michelin star specifically is, it's like the Oscars of cooking. It's what some chefs strive their whole lives for, and judging by my reaction, I could've cared less, but in my defense, I didn't know what it meant to have a Michelin star. For me, it could've just been a pat on the back because that's what it felt like.

Days went by and things started to change. People were coming into the restaurant but this time it was a new crowd and the whole place had a new feel. I had people coming from all over to try my food, and it was all because of this star. At no point at all did I think some newspaper articles and interviews would give my business the boom it so desperately needed. It wasn't just the amount of people coming that gave me satisfaction, it was how my compliments were beginning to change. They all went from the friendly, "This plate is delicious," or "This is an amazing chef," which I appreciated each time, to people telling me that my food was the best thing they've ever had in their lives.

To me that's what it's all about because if I can cook something that can impact people in such a powerful way, then I know all these sacrifices are worth it.

That prophecy came to life when I met this couple who told me the wife and daughter were having troubles and no therapist could solve them. I truly believe that food can solve all issues, so I invited the woman to bring her daughter in to eat and see how their problems would be resolved. The next week they came, and sure enough, they worked things out. I wouldn't say we were the best of friends, but in a sense, a strong bond was built between us. A few months later, I got a call from the lady who had actually been hospitalized for some time. "Carlos can I ask you for a favor?" she said.

I quickly responded, "Of course, anything, what do you need?" In a weak voice she said, "I'm really craving a chicken soup. Could you please make one? But, please, make it the best soup you've ever made. My husband will come by soon to pick it up."

I quickly assured her that I'd be more than happy to make that soup for her, and I would personally bring it over. As I hung up the phone—and I don't know how I put myself in these situations—I came to the conclusion that I've never made a chicken soup. I don't even think I even really ever had one. So here I was promising this sick lady that I would make her the best chicken soup she ever tasted but had no idea where to begin. So, I prayed to God that by His will He would make this the best chicken soup ever, and I winged it. I dropped off the soup and crossed my fingers it would do her justice. Little did I know weeks later this lady passed, and one of her last wishes was to eat chicken soup and that I was the person she wanted to make that wish come true.

This is what I woke up every morning for and worked hour after hour and lost sleep over. This moment, to be able to give her one her last meal, made everything worth it. I think that some people forget that if a chef is truly being a chef and truly investing his time into his meals, he sprinkles his story—that is a part of him—into every dish. Perhaps that is the most important ingredient of all.

If I were to give anyone a key point on what it is to be a chef it would be to have passion, to not be greedy and look for a new life, to put your will in God and trust it.

That's what I did. I didn't search for celebrity status or a million-dollar paycheck. No, I didn't come to the United States with a vision of being highly successful.

I came with a goal to be different.

CHEF ATZIMBA PÉREZ

—

2
Passion

My name is Atzimba Perez, and I was born in Ciudad Hidalgo Michoacán. One thing you should know: I love to cook.

The method of coating each particular ingredient in the special seasonings of our lives, our cultures, who we were really are, is what I characterize myself most with. As I sprinkle the spices on each one of my dishes, they no longer just serve the purpose of decoration or keeping a dish from being plain, their flavor now symbolizes a country as a whole and the life events within a family in each one of our homes.

Food was never just an ordinary necessity. It was something that

I found beauty and art in. My love of food started in middle school in our kitchen and transcended into my high school days. It formed the base of my concentration for further studies and a future career in gastronomy and hospitality in college in Morelia. Not only did I focus my energy and time into food, but I also went on and pushed myself further to be able to incorporate the use of the Italian and English languages to further boost my cultural understanding and complement the gift I was about to deliver to the world.

From then on, I always characterized myself by my passion for the things that I did, the things I believed in.

It was no secret that I had loved cooking and anything that had to do with gastronomy and food and just the overall enhancement of life that food brought to me. From those strong feelings came the ones that continuously erupted in me—so much that they could not be pushed aside for anyone. This is the job where I was always the boss in charge of the vision I wanted to carry out what my outcome could be.

In the technical provisional college of Mexico, I studied the overall marketing and promotion of gastronomy from all over Mexico. My studies led me to participate in two very important culinary contests. I dealt with many days of stress and worry in order to accomplish the events. My hard work paid off because when the day finally arrived, they announced me as the winner.

I decided to open a bakery in the town that I grew up in, mostly because it was the town that I knew. The town had familiar faces that already knew me, and the location was too good to miss. Thankfully, by the grace of God, my business boomed. Of course, I had those customers, the ones who always ordered the same thing without hesitation and without blinking their eyes, as well as the ones who would have the exact amount of cash balled up in their fidgety palms even before you politely told them their total. But then of course, there were others, the regulars, who came because of my international cakes whether it was Swedish, French or Italian.

I was lucky enough to have people who not only believed in my dream but who continuously came and supported it.

Coming from a broken household, having some form of stability whether it be personal or not means a lot. My mom didn't have an occupation that exactly paid all the bills the way we wanted to, and it didn't exactly provide enough for lavish gifts or even any gifts in reality, and I remember counting the days down in the kitchen where I could just forget my worries and live with my uncles for a few days. I loved being with them because being with them meant being away from the world. I spent so many days just surrounded by the simple things in life: the air, the sky, the earth, the grass I played with, the animals, and the stacks of wood that were meant to keep us warm. These simple things made my heart beat. Not only does my heart smile because of the natural world I was able to experience but because being there was just another extension of my culinary adventure.

My uncles and aunts taught me how to make cheese and how to make tamales. They showed me how to make the most delicious basic Mexican dishes that only a special touch can turn from ordinary to extraordinary. For me, this was the best time as I loved being in tune with the natural world around me; I loved putting my hands on things and feeling them. I was making something in the most literal way.

My mom worked with my aunt who also made her business

preparing food and selling it to others for special events. Even though I wasn't the only one with a culinary passion, I was the only one who really seemed to be utilizing my passion the way *I* wanted. My family seemed to be tied down by the simmering of pans, the harsh affixation of chili flakes traveling through the air and down into the windpipes causing a nonstop cough. It was no longer something that enriched them because it became another duty instead of a gift.

I refused to let that be my future. I refused to let my passion turn into an obligatory task that physically and mentally drained me.

It was hard for me to decide what I wanted to do because after my parents divorced, I was stuck with my two siblings and my father. Our little family became closer, though, especially my father and me. I was both his little girl, yet I also took over all the motherly duties, and for all these years of my life, I never really left my father's side. When I tell you that I adore my family, I truly do. There is, however, a very special bond that my father and I share and having to leave him was among the hardest things I've ever had to do. I can still hear his voice the day I decided to leave. He said to me, "You have to promise me one thing, please never abandon me . . . never leave me alone."

It wasn't just a literal plea because we both understood that I had to leave, but it meant more symbolically because you can leave something or someone but still always have them with you and vice versa—they will always have you with them too.

I think what my father meant . . . actually . . . what I know he meant was that it's very easy to forget one's roots, to start all over and flip the page and forget the whole story that brought you to this moment, to forget the foundation that started it all.

So that's what I always try to do. I try to continue cooking meals that represented home to me, like my mom's pozole or the guava tamales that reminded me of happiness and joy when they popped up in local carnivals. I try never to forget the values of hard work and love that were bestowed upon me no matter how my life changes for the better or worse because I know all of these little things make me.

I often get asked if I ever regret anything I've done or the way that I've done things or the sacrifices I've made. My answer is simple: not everything has been absolutely worth it. From leaving my homeland at the age of nineteen, pregnant, to watching my first born battle through bronchitis in his first days of life, to then being sent back over six times just so that I could be able to grant my children that American citizenship. It's difficult to see why anyone would think that the passage to this land is *la vie en rose* when it's not. There's always criticism surrounding you. Whether it is because of your personal choices or things that you cannot control such as who you are mentally, physically, spiritually or ethnically.

And it's not just local people who are different than you. Sometimes it's your own people, and I think that's the hardest thing for me to comprehend. Sometimes, the people that you would expect to have the most compassion for you end up being consumed by jealousy. I think that's what can happen with us. We can get so greedy that it's hard for us to see other people succeeding and instead of cheering them on and helping them out, we are too concerned with our status and wondering how we can win the race before they do.

To anybody who is to confront judgment like this, I say, "Live your life with passion, consistency, and hard work because in the face of fear and all the obstacles that life throws at you, where there is a passion burning eminently within your heart not even the sea can tame it."

TRES LECHES CAKE

By Atzimba Perez

Ingredients:
9 egg yolks
9 egg whites
1 teaspoon baking powder
1 cup of granulated sugar
2 cups of all-purpose flour
1 cup of sour cream
1 cup of condensed milk
1 cup of evaporated milk
1 cup rompope (Mexican Style Eggnog)

Cream:
1 lb. of strawberries
2 cups of heavy whipping cream
2 teaspoons of powder sugar

Instructions:
1. Preheat oven to 330 degrees – grease a 10" round or square metal baking pan with butter and sprinkle a little flour.

2. Beat the eggs yolks for 5 minutes then add 1 cup of sugar. Separately, combine dry ingredients in a bowl (flour and baking powder).

3. Beat eggs whites until soft peaks form.

4. Fold eggs yolks into the dry ingredients and eggs whites

5. Pour mixture into the baking pan. Bake at 330 degrees for 40 minutes. Let it cool for 20 minutes.

6. Blend the sour cream, condensed milk, evaporated milk and rompope in a blender.

7. Cut cake in half horizontally and pour the milk mixture on both cake half's

8. In a bowl beat the heavy cream with the powder sugar. Build the cake by placing the cream in the middle of the cake and then frost the cake with cream. Add strawberries for flavor and décor.

CHEF CÉSAR PINEDA

3
Love of Learning

If there was ever a more ironic picture of a bad boy who does good, it would be me. Not in the sense that I'm really bad, but my actions may be called crazy. It's justified to call them so because they are; everything I have done has not been "by the book"—yet I really hate breaking the rules . . . My name is Cesar Pineda, and at sixteen I left my home. I left my country, I left the world and the lifestyle I was brought up in and accustomed to, and I started fresh in a country where I knew nothing, where I had no life and no family.

I grew up in Venezuela, a country that has no comparison to the catastrophe that is now happening in my country today. I grew up walking to the butcher shop with my grandma as the coveted favorite nephew. In the intimate space of my very own home, I dined with world leaders, vice presidents and diplomats. I have loving parents who guaranteed me the world and provided it for me. All of this happened in an unrecognizable land of beauty that once was. I come from Italian and Venezuelan descent, and my grandfather immigrated to the United States from Italy in the fifties because Venezuela was the land of opportunity. Accompanying its oil boom, I had the chance to live in one of the grand "meccas" of cultural and humanistic diversity.

I grew up knowing the taste of curry in an environment where I was encouraged to discover the world around me, where exploring was as accessible as crossing the street. I grew up lucky and fortunate, and I never take that for granted because I remember it every day.

My mother was the key component in leading me where I wanted to go. She made sure that my siblings and I were always hungry for learning—both literal and metaphorical hunger. If it wasn't Mexican food this day then it was Greek food the next day, and if it wasn't that, then it was Peruvian food or whatever the world had to offer. My tongue never had the chance to become picky because I refused to let it. If you would see me now, you would understand why.

I could never be picky; I love food. It had come from the push and the drive that my mother had for immersing us through all kinds of seasonings and spices, through the textures of other cultures.

But none of this world discovery could compare to the classic seafood dish my mother prepared for us. My father was a pharmaceutical professional and his pharmacy was right on the bay of one of the biggest ports in Caracas, Venezuela. Here, he got to learn about marine life and befriend local fishermen. Those friendships provided for us, and we would get gifts of giant shrimp and fish. It was the funniest thing to see my stout little Venezuelan mother carrying a huge fish—you didn't know who was walking who! It's safe to say I lived a close to perfect life.

I can't complain, but all of that changed once I hit mid-adolescence. I do have to point out that even though I was very privileged in many ways, I never expected anything to come for free. I understood the harsh reality behind the connection of hard work and pay of working to survive because I think a part of me was prepared for a future that I had no idea was destined to become my own. I think that mentality was the driving force behind my next plan of action. As I said, mid-adolescence were not the easiest years for me, and I hit a wall of miscommunication and an overall feeling of being misunderstood. It got to the point where I just felt the urge to escape . . . so I did. I took what little was mine and rode a bus to the embassy where I, in a sense, smuggled myself into a foreign country. Of course, being underage, there was paperwork that needed to be signed by some sort of guardian since at that time I needed to apply for a visa that I didn't have, but given my circumstances that wasn't possible. So what did I do? I forged every piece of paper required, and when the day for takeoff came, I told the lady at the front that my nonexistent mother at the moment was looking for a parking spot and sent me first, and with that, ladies and gentlemen, I was on a plane to my new home with a buddy of mine.

I arrived in Chicago on December 16. Imagine a sixteen-year-old Venezuelan kid fighting against cold conditions and harsh winds that ignorance did not prepare him for. I spoke no lick of English outside of "hello" and "my name is" upon my arrival, but even that did not stop me from moving forward. I worked many jobs, and I loved each one.

Each one was a different experience, a different chance for me to learn and grow, and I think who I am today comes from each one of those experiences.

People learned that if I was to work for them, it was going to be good—that I wasn't some young punk looking to make a quick dollar, and that not only made good connections but also brought a sense of integrity and pride to my being.

Because, here I was, free. I was paying for my own transportation and apartment. I was making it on my own and suddenly realizing that maybe I wasn't wasting my time after all.

At one point I worked for an Italian family that I loved, considering they treated me like family. They owned a huge bank, and my buddy and I worked together for them. I explicitly remember one day working a huge banquet the owner typically held for New Year celebrations. It was a long running night, and we didn't get off until much later. I finished what I had to do and started heading back home. Now, the only problem was that I didn't consider that in that specific location, buses didn't run after a certain hour. I was about to become the first Venezuelan human popsicle in the splintering cold. The first building I tried to get into was closed, so I found the nearest twenty-four-hour Dunkin Donuts and called it home for the night until I was able to get picked up by my buddy the very next day. That night taught me a very valuable lesson that still holds true for me today: always live close to your job.

As time went by, I got the chance to travel to many Latino

countries. Here, I was enjoying my life, not really thinking about much, until I realized my visa was moments from expiration. Once that day hit, Illinois became my forever home. Luckily, I've never experienced any type of first-hand discrimination from it, but it would probably be one of the hardest battles I've had to overcome just holding the fact that I was illegal—that I wasn't supposed to be here. For me, that was so much tougher because I hate breaking the rules. So, just living with that paranoia that I could get stopped by a policeman haunted me.

It was equally tough once I decided to open up my business. It was never easy opening up *"Ciao Amore."*

It was a struggle from the beginning, but I always remembered to hold on to the future, to what my next step was going to create and become, and to not let go of that no matter what the circumstance.

Experiencing what I did and bearing the obstacles I did, made me want to help others more—to really hold true the humility that my mother so engraved into my being. That's why whenever I can, I take in the local kids of Chicago's Pilsen neighborhood, those who don't have parents to guide them. I happily take them in, and when they say it's their time to go, I leave them with a smile knowing that I did everything I could to bestow the gift God has lent me.

At one point, I knew the success Ciao Amore was taking, and if one of the younger kids was not working, then unfortunately they were told to go because in my kitchen there was no room, no time to waste on those who didn't want to make this dream work.

It's been a long and tiring journey to reach the point where I am now. I don't think I would trade it for any other because behind this came growth and an even stronger passion for cooking than I could ever imagine, a passion that has given me the opportunity to unite my family.

Never once did my sixteen-year- old self believe that I would be sitting here discussing with anyone my story of success or the loneliness of my struggles or even eventually bringing my family along with me.

Here's to life, here's to dreams, here's to the future.

HALLACAS CARAQUEÑAS
By César Pineda

Hallacas Caraqueñas
Two kilos of precooked white corn flour
4 pounds of meat to cook
4 pounds of pork leg (much better leg)
2 pounds peeled tomatoes
5 big anions
2 large leeks cleaned and peeled
8 red bell peppers
8 green bell peppers
2 cups of stuffed green olives
1 cup of capers
1 cup of raisins
4 cups of red table wine
1 cup of peeled almonds
1 bunch of celery
1/2 cup of sugar
2 heads of garlic
1 1/2 cup chicken broth
Achiote (annatto) to give yellow color to the mass

Flat washed banana leaves.
4 cups of chicken broth for the dough mix.

For garnish
Red bell peppers in strips. Julienne cut onions. Shredded chicken breast (previously boiled). Green olives and raisins.

Stew Directions

1. Cut the onions, red and green bell peppers and tomatoes into cubes.

2. Smash garlic. Finely chop celery and leek.

3. Cut all the meat into small pieces.

4. In a large pot, put about 4 oz. of oil, add the wine and sugar. Add all the meat until it is all sealed

5. Add all the chopped vegetables, salt and spices to taste.

6. Cook over medium heat until everything is cooked and the mixture has thickened.

7. Put aside letting it cool down before starting to assemble the hallacas.

Dough for the Hallacas

1. In a mixing bowl put the yellow corn flour, chicken broth, cooked annatto and salt. And mix it until all ingredients are soft and integrated.

2. On a clean table, make cut squares out of the banana leaves, grease each of them with a mixture of oil and annatto placing a ball of dough on the center of each leave extending it gently with your hands until is all flat.

3. Grab a portion of the stew and put it on the center of the dough.

4. Garnish with 7 pieces of raisins, olives, a couple of almonds, capers, julienne onions, red bell pepper strips.

5. Close your hallacas with a strong yarn and steamed for one hour or until your hallacas are cooked.

CHEF MARIBEL MOLINA CORTES

Totopos Restaurant

—

4
Curiosity

It's only natural that a child questions everything, to have an innate need for why or what something is. For most children the conversation typically goes something like this:

Innocent question: "Why do dogs bark?"

Followed by polite answer: "So that they can communicate with each other."

Follow-up question: "But why?"

Further thought-out response: "Well, because dogs can't talk, and barking is the only way that they can understand one another..."

Further deliberated question: "...but why?"

Rather annoyed response: "Well, because they just do."
Accepting, yet unsatisfied nod.
End of conversation.

As a child—even as a young adult—my questions were not that much different, but they often lacked variation. Through days of hard work and sleepless nights, my mind stayed fixated on one single question: What is it like to be Daddy's little girl? And how does one make a daddy stay? Did I make Daddy leave? Who made him leave . . . and why did he leave?

I know, it's not the usual thoughts racing around a little girl's head, but then again, I wasn't living the life of a usual little girl, or at least I wasn't living the life I had imagined for myself. A life where I could walk home to both parents who asked how my day had been, to which I would respond gleefully, waving colored worksheets and holographic gold stars, and boast as only a young heart in second grade can. But not everyone is granted this, no matter how many gold stars you get.

And, maybe those are the same thoughts that raced around my father's head as he silently folded his clothes into a worn suitcase that was already itching for its next trip and took his final steps crossing the door. Maybe this wasn't the life he had imagined for himself either. Maybe my mother wasn't the wife he had dreamed of, maybe it was the kids . . . me? Maybe, it was the way I didn't always listen the first time around or how sometimes I would stay out to play just a little longer than I was supposed to. Maybe he was just having a bad day, or he took a walk and got lost or took the wrong turn home. Maybe his legs began to weaken under the weight of the suitcase's smooth leather handles and he questioned his actions just before it was too late.

Maybe, just maybe, he looked back before he shut the door on all of us and almost took it all back . . .

But, I can't be sure. And in a world of so many maybes, I can only hold on to the things that I know to be true.

In second grade, I loved my dad, and I thought he loved me too. I was under the impression that he would always be there to protect me. I believed his every word and every promise unconditionally, like only a woman could for the man she loves, but then, he left.

And never came back.

There is no maybe on this point. It is what I know.

Life has a funny way of unfolding itself, and one of the things it never failed to show me is how nothing stays the same.

I was no longer a little girl. Granted, I was the oldest amongst three girls and a boy, but I at least felt like I had some form of childhood to call my own.

Following my father's departure, my years of innocence were also taken from me. Instead, my days consisted of waking up at 4:00 a.m. to help my mom with her locally-owned business, and I got a new later bedtime that probably sounded more exciting than it what it really turned out to be. I was no longer playing "house" with my dolls, I was living it. I was now put in a head position in my household. I never asked for much. Not only was I the big sister, but I was also the mom too. If we wanted to eat, I cooked for my siblings. I cleaned the home. I did the laundry. I attempted to pretend our broken home could be whole again.

They say a perfect person, a perfect child, is impossible to come across, but I was damn close to being one.

Just as life has its way of changing things, so did my perfect attitude. . . it was somewhere in the transition into adolescence that a spark ignited in me in which I had given myself the task of recuperating every ounce of childhood I had lost. I wasn't the worst kid to ever live, but I definitely entered a somewhat rebellious stage as is expected in most teenagers. The only reason this is somewhat surprising is because it's coming from the girl who felt like she was turning thirty on her tenth birthday.

Some of the most significant moments in high school I remember are some of the pranks I used to help execute, which, now that I look back on it, I can't help but at least feel a little bad for my teachers— but that was probably the last thing I was feeling back then. The best prank was when our teacher would casually go on with his lesson, and as soon as he turned around, one of us would, as silently as possible, sneak one by one out the back door of the classroom.

I don't know what the hardest part of the game was, attempting to stifle our desperate chuckles or making it out of the door within those seven seconds our teacher would face the board. The best part though, was those moments of adrenaline when the heat from your boiling blood streamed from your fingertips and reached your ears. That moment when you zoned out completely from your classmates' buzz, and the rush you felt when you reached outside along with the others who snuck out before you. You couldn't help but die of laughter as one by one your classroom grew smaller and smaller and your teacher's confusion grew more and more.

These were amongst the best moments I've had.
Why? Because these were the moments where I felt truly free.

But, as I've said many times before, life gets in the way and changes everything around. It wasn't much later that I had to make a tough choice again, putting aside my emotions for the betterment of the family.

At the age of 22, and alongside my then husband, I decided I would fly over to the United States to find a job that could provide me with better pay so that I could better help my mom and fulfill my then dream of opening a school that concentrated on children with special needs.

I knew that this was the right thing to do, but a part of me couldn't help but feel at least a little resentment. After all, it was another moment in which it was me who was sacrificing time in order to sustain the unity of this family. I just didn't know why it had to be me (but secretly I knew it had to be me). It's in moments like these when I do remember the slight moments I had with my father and how he always used to tell me that I wasn't "part of the bunch," meaning I wasn't like the rest of my family. The reason was simple: I constantly had to push myself to stand out and be different so that I could prove to those around me who I truly was.

The stay in the U.S. was a temporary plan, just enough time for me to get situated and earn enough to really start my life, maybe a few years or so, but by the time two years passed in our new foreign home, everything had changed.

Arriving here wasn't like setting up my own home. I checked in as a housewife who was constantly being taken care of, and it's not as if I was ungrateful that my husband was able to take care of the majority of my needs, it's just that that kind of life wasn't me.

I had never been in a situation where I didn't have to work for what I wanted much less in a situation where I wasn't able to. I was in a foreign country in which I knew zero percent of the language, so I grew completely dependent on my husband. Plus, my only worry in the world was my daughter, and since I was already given the position of housewife, I didn't find the need to speak the language if I was just going to be home anyway.

My husband would go to work, and I would stay and take care of my daughter—attend to the home basically. So, I decided that if I was going to be a housewife, I was going to be the best housewife I could be. My life at this point seemed to be made, but I can't deny that there wasn't this subtle tug in my heart that try hard as I might to be satisfied with what life had given me thus far, I just wasn't. I'm not sure if it was the voice of my mother reminding me of the value of work and how to always work hard because it's only through work that doors open or if it was the voice telling me that I wasn't like "the bunch," and that I was worth so much more than a glorified modern-day Cinderella with no glass slipper (unless glass cleaner counts as a substitute).

It wasn't until one day when my ex-husband and I went out to eat, as we usually did, that I had a little burst of hope and determination emerge inside of me. Within the time that we habituated into our new home, there were two main things that stood out to me. One was that there were not very many authentic Mexican or for that matter Latino restaurants around, and two, that they pretty much all sucked . . . badly. While reflecting on this issue, something took me over body and soul, and suddenly my mouth was telling my ex-husband that I was going to open my own restaurant—before I had any time to really think about what I just burdened myself with. I think my ex-husband was just as shocked as I was and simply replied with a slight chuckle, telling me how crazy I was. Maybe he was right actually.

Maybe I was crazy for wanting to suddenly create something I had no prior experience with, but soon it dawned on me that this wasn't just a cry into the wind. No, this restaurant was going to be my home—made by me for me and my daughter.

Along with many things, even love doesn't always last. Sometimes the priest's riveting words, "for better or for worse," just aren't enough, and they weren't. As I sensed the bond that we had made slowly loosening its hold, I began taking English classes. This would unexpectedly be the beginning of everything, and in efforts to prepare myself for my next future, I walked along this back road right by the lake, when I finally saw it. Almost like one of those flippy books that page by page reveals gradual increments of movement drawn out in order to create a nostalgic motion picture. That is exactly what I saw as I looked at this vacant building as much more than just what it appeared to be but what it had the potential of being. I could see the twinkly lights imitating the Chicago night stars and imagined the afternoons where we'd convert it into a tiny café, and I heard the live music of a local band bouncing off of customers' laughter and chatter along with smelling the day's roast simmering in its pot, and I couldn't help but just smile in my own solitude.

I continued to attend my English classes purposefully, taking this little road every time just so that I had an excuse to dream of my little place, until one day on a day like any other, I witnessed something that made my heart drop. It seems as if I wasn't the only dreamer who was inspired by this location, and just like that, my restaurant was no longer mine but someone else's who was actually able to make their dreams work for them.

The crashes and burns soon followed suit as my husband and I decided to divorce, and then after ten long years, my boss and I were fired from the location where we were. He was able to write me a recommendation letter with which I later found work for a cleaning company. It wasn't much later that a lady that worked with me contacted one of my daughter's uncles and suggested to him that we open up a restaurant. He quickly was open to the idea, and when they asked me, I couldn't help but to take a moment to analyze what I would be getting myself into at that point. At last, my dream was catching up to me. I figured I had some savings, so why not? And so began the beginning of everything.

It seems as though restaurant hunting was even more difficult than house hunting. There is that constant anxiousness of just wanting to start your business at that moment and wanting to take whatever you can, yet there's also a logistical side of finding the best place with a selling location. My daughter's uncle had found a place that fit well within our budget, but the place was basically vacant. As in, everything would have to be constructed from scratch in order to be transformed into a restaurant.

I ended up deciding it wouldn't benefit me in any manner to pursue this plan, so I put a "no" on my behalf, and it was left at that. About a week later, the lady I worked with and I received a call from my daughter's uncle telling us about another place that was available, and that it was a bit small, but we could afford it.

Once I set foot in this location it was a done deal.

I knew my search was over and that this was the place for me, no question about it. It's as if my restaurant dream that was asleep within in me had sprung into full force once I entered this place.

It wasn't easy though, I grew up only cooking for myself and my other family members, so having to take care of strangers was a completely different task I never had to face before. It was especially challenging at times in the beginning when we first started, and we would have to serve up to eighty people, and I would just stand there asking myself what in the world I was going to do.

On top of that, our grand opening was anything but easy. As my daughter's uncle was the only one who truly knew anything about running the business, and was the one who was teaching us anything and everything. The whole plan was working out great until he said that he wanted to hurry up with setup and logistics and open before he returned to Mexico.

I was astonished. There was absolutely no time to do that, and try as hard as I might to fight for my stance, he basically pushed me to learn along the way. It was definitely complete chaos those first few weeks in which we opened, but we just kept trudging along. Although times were tough, I felt like it could only get better from that point until my cofounder decided to quit. She was helping with the children at home, and her husband was asking for the supposed money she would be making to help pay for the house—money that she wasn't receiving as we were barely starting. She could understand that even if her husband couldn't, so there was no other option for her but to go. So, I quickly became in charge of the whole kitchen seven days a week. I was taking care of everything and even though providing for my daughter and needing to make my dream succeed kept me going, at a certain point, it just wasn't enough.

Like when I laid bedridden in a fluorescent lit hospital room due to a stroke induced by all the stress and energy my job was consuming. It had gotten to the point where I wasn't even able to attend church at all nor was I able to tend to my daughter in the way that she so deserved. After all, this was all for her. The doctor told me that I needed to lighten my load because I was literally killing myself slowly. When the doctor's words hit me, I realized that he was right and that I needed to make some major changes. It was as if being close to death, even just by warning, was enough to want to start all over. From that day on, my restaurant was not open on Sundays, ever. I decided to leave the work to God on those days and focus my time on Him and my daughter.

This has been among my best decisions, as both of these people have proven to be the reason I even am who I am today. The Lord continuously showed off his grace toward me in extraordinary ways that only he can do. I remember the moment I was so stressed about not being able to pay off the restaurant bills and seeing how just like a pesky ant invasion, they kept coming and coming. I remember praying to the Lord and asking him to help me in any way possible because I had no clue where I was going to round this money up. The next day, when I went in to open the envelope, I received a total bill amount of $5 for my restaurant. And I don't need anything to prove it for me because I already know it was Him, as it always has been.

My daughter, on the other hand, has been like my shining armor per se. I think one of the scariest parts of living here as an immigrant is that you're always battling fears with everything and everyone, especially the language.

For instance, on one occasion, my daughter overheard my English teacher telling us that we needed to practice our English more by utilizing it in our everyday speech. Then, I went to the store where I proceeded to give my daughter a slight nudge to let her know I needed her help in order to ask a question. "Definitely," she answered, "but no more because your teacher said you need to practice, and until you do, I'm not going to help you anymore." From that point I did, though it was broken English. I owe it to her for breaking that wall of insecurity that I had in order to get here.

As time goes by, I often reflect back on my life and think of all the things that could've happened if life would have happened just a little differently—if there would've been someone there to tell me to have more courage and to seek the Lord wholeheartedly because under His guidance anything is possible. As I think of all this, I realize that everything that life has handed me is because I'm not "part of the bunch." I was made to challenge every obstacle put in my way and prove my worth.

My name is Maribel Molina, and these are the things I know.

MOLE DE EPAZOTE

By Maribel Molina Cortes

Mole of Epazote

5 to 6 pieces of chicken
3 large tomatoes
5 chipotle peppers
Garlic and onions
2 Zucchinis
5 leaves of epazote
Salt

1. Wash the chicken very well. Put it in the pot to cover the chicken with water, and make sure it is completely covered.

2. Boil it and add garlic onions and salt.

3. In a separate container, boil chipotle and tomatoes.

4. When tomatoes look cooked, take off water and put in mixer with garlic, onions and salt and a little bit of water, enough to make the sauce.

5. When chicken is cooked, add sauce and epazote leaves and zucchini that have been washed and cut (long slices or round slices- not too thin) cover the pot and boil for 5-10 minutes on low heat.

Ready to serve.

CHEF AMADOR JIMÉNEZ
Casa Blanca Restaurant

—

5
Honesty

You know that saying "be a man?" Well, I don't really know what that means because personally, I would much rather be a woman. Now, let me finish that statement before it becomes misinterpreted. That doesn't entail the stereotypical definition of the female gender, the one where people think a woman is too afraid to break a nail or get her hands dirty. That a woman is too preoccupied over her beauty sleep to stay up working late or that the build of a woman's bones is only meant to sustain childbirth and other household needs, but could never withstand the weight of the real world, much less have the strength to keep up with it. No. The notion that a woman must depend on a man or that a woman needs a man in order to be something is a silly thought because clearly those under this presumption have never met the woman I grew up with, the woman that I came to know clearly as my mother.

The fact is that this is a woman who has the means to give a man so much more than his biological makeup. It was not just her blood running through his veins. It was not just the food from her womb that aided in his formation, but it was everything that she was and that she lost that made that man—me—who he is today.

My life has never been as pretty as the words I inadvertently streamed together up above. It's been tough and uncertain. For instance, my home life wasn't even certain due to the constant movement of our family from one town to another. I never really had anything that was reliable. My family life was always difficult as we moved from the city of Michoacán, Mexico, to a little city called Ulan and it was when I was 5 and parents split that I finally gained certainty. The certainty that my mom was the only thing set in my life. So, along with my three other brothers and sisters, my mom took us under her wing because she had no other choice.

She taught us that in life you always have a choice but to choose wisely—because as soon as you do, you will always carry the responsibility of whatever your choices bring.

My mother did not choose to be a woman—that was something only God gave her, but as a woman, she chose to marry my father just like she chose to carry his children, and she chose to push and sacrifice and kill to push those children along because they were her responsibility. She pushed her body and her bones to a near breaking point, and she never once cried over the sharp pains that shot through her joints like strategically placed missile fires. Though she wasn't one to complain over whatever card life dealt her, *I* could see the pain in her eyes when her reassuring smile engulfed my aura telling me everything was going to be okay.

What? Did you expect a woman like that to showcase any type of weakness? Of course not! But even her facade of omniscience was quickly overturned by the evident wariness in her walk or the way her eyelids struggled to find the energy to continue playing awake. I noticed all this partly because all my time was spent with my family, either working hand-in-hand or brainstorming new ideas to provide for the home.

By the age of nine, I probably had held more jobs than most middle-aged men. I had no shame in this. I had to do it to help keep my family going. Seeing how far my mom would go in order to make sure we received a better life than she had was all I needed to keep me going.

I helped sell certain things in the home. I looked for strangers to help carry their bags—basically anything that could be turned into a job, I did. I also loved it because in a way, it was my way of being entertained, given that we didn't really have much else.

I'm not exactly sure what my feelings are of childhood because looking back at it now, I realize I never really had one. All that moving around erased the memories a child would normally have. There was never a possibility to construct any form of bond with people when you knew you were due to leave at any day. My days consisted solely of work, no real traditional fun. So, instead, I made it fun. Of course, I saw other kids with their television sets displaying light shows through sheer chiffon curtains on Friday nights or even kids having the time to play without a care in mind. I just watched from afar.

I was never jealous; I just wondered what my purpose was.

We were all good kids due to the way my mom raised us. Her mentality and her thoughts were that there should always be good food to eat and one should always have a good role model to follow. In this case, for us, it was her. At a very young age, we were taught the value of honesty, hard work, and responsibility; it was part of all our moral clothing, especially considering that within us as a family, we all watched out for each other. My mother implemented this almost train-like system: the oldest sibling would watch the youngest, the second oldest the second youngest, and so on and so forth, but I was the youngest so who did I watch over?

Well, that's the thing, no one.

Now, this wasn't always a good thing. It could really go two ways. On one hand, I had more liberty because I wasn't preoccupied over someone else. but it also gave me more opportunities to make silly mistakes. As I said previously, I was a pretty responsible kid. I took care of my duties. I followed the rules when they were told to me, but sometimes following the rules did not produce an expected outcome. Unfortunately, being someone who is considered poor or of an underprivileged background tends to bring out the worst in people. It's common for people to automatically assume that people who aren't as fortunate as them are thieves, crooks and just overall bad people, but that's not always the case. Sometimes life deals a card that certain individuals aren't prepared to handle. People who struggle might turn to desperate methods that start to convert them into people who they themselves don't even recognize, and I think that's what people don't understand.

Especially now with immigrants being the hot topic on everyone's tongues, we are often looked at through a very narrow window that's either black or white, but that's not who we are. We are colors and dancing pigments rolling off our tongues. We are today, tomorrow and yesterday, all encased in the energy and vivacity only our ancestors could've passed down. But, we have since then migrated into foreign lands that don't feel like home and most definitely don't always treat us like home. We are often pushed down the ladder and end up at the bottom of the food chain in which my people—your people—act in ways that don't resonate with our inner values.

When we were young, we would go to the local markets and spend our time kicking through the sand and catching a glimmer or two of knickknacks we knew we couldn't afford. One day, my friend caught a glimpse of a very nice gold ring. It wasn't very expensive, but considering there was barely enough money for food, a gold ring was out of the question. It might've been something in the sly smile slowly creeping onto his face that linked two and two together, but whatever it was, I knew it wasn't good.

I remember his body slowly molding itself into a cool calm kid just looking for a potential gift and how the sun refracted off of its golden sheen while he slowly flipped it back and forth through his fading innocent hands, as if it were a fresh clump of silly putty. If you were another outside spectator, you would barely notice his eyes darting back and forth, almost forcing them past the ability of his peripheral vision in order to catch any onlookers. He kept rolling his ankle to mask the absolute fear boiling inside him. All of this, to anyone, would have gone unnoticed, but to me, they were like flashing marquee lights yelling "stop." My feeling of dread only grew stronger once he, in a pleasant voice quickly whispered, "Hey I need you to keep lookout for me, yeah?"

In that moment, I really don't remember giving a definite response. On one hand, I was in shock given the situation we were in. For the other part, I was this little kid knowing my friend was about to do something wrong and not wanting to turn him in, but also having my mother's all too familiar voice in the back of my head reminding me of everything she had taught me and that I would now violating if I were to go along with this. Eventually it was too much to handle, and I did end up listening to my mother. I tried to stop my friend and tell the store clerk, but in an odd turn of events, my friend was able to get away, and the store clerk caught me with a ring in hand under the presumption that I was trying to steal. At this thought, the man grabbed my hand and wouldn't let go against all of my pleading. My body quickly transitioned into panic mode where my only thought was "You need to get out of here." Through a lot of effort on my behalf, I was able to wriggle my hand out of his grasp but with the ring still in my hand.

I would just like to clarify that I, in no case, was trying to steal the ring. Actually, I was very much attempting to do the exact opposite, but, as a child who felt like they just escaped their impending doom, the only thing on my mind was getting my legs to run faster so I could get home. The adrenaline was fun, but the line between adrenaline and fear got very blurred in this instance.

Also, it seems to me that all the odds were stacked against me this day because one thing that everyone who has ever grown up in a small town knows is that some way somehow everyone ends up knowing everyone else, so good luck getting away with anything—ever.

The owner of the store actually ended up coming to my house and telling my mom everything, obviously leaving out the part where I didn't intentionally attempt to steal the ring, but that's beside the point. Well, to make a long story short, my mother closed the door and asked me if I stole the ring, to which I hesitantly replied, "Yes," even though it wasn't completely true, I technically did steal it. Whether it was on purpose or not didn't matter to my mother. The thing that did matter to her was the fact that did it, and that, all by itself, was bad enough for her.

If you want to know why I even bothered telling this story, it is because of this right here: that day has become an unforgettable memory in my life. My mom, yes, used to hit us as part of our discipline, but the one thing she never did was hit us in the face. Everything below that, though, was fair game. That day my mom's rule was thrown out the window, and when she was done, there was no way of hiding the marks she had left on me, and her reasoning is something I will never forget.

My mom looked at me and said, "Now you know I never even so much as touched your face, but I want you to remember this. I want people to be able to see these marks and have no other choice but to ask what happened, and to this you'll have no other choice but to tell them what you've done. I hope that you feel enough embarrassment and shamefulness to make you think twice before taking something that is not yours, something that you did not work for."

Facing the consequences of my actions and taking only the things I earn is something that I hold near and dear to my heart and that I have tried to incorporate in my daily life.

Reaching the age of twenty, I was still under the mentality in which I, in essence, did not really matter. I mean this in the sense that whatever it took to help push my family along is what I was going to do, and if that meant sacrificing time and energy, so be it. Selfishness was just a luxury I was not willing to invest in.

At this point, I was working for the La Canada shoe company based in Mexico where I had spent many long hours pushing myself through the ranks of the company. I enjoyed my job and had contributed so much to the company, that they eventually sent me to the United States on behalf of the company to learn English. I arrived directly in Chicago and was welcomed by a brother that I already had here. I guess it always makes a change a little easier by having someone you know with you, but quickly I came to experience the fast-paced hustle and bustle of this country.

I lived with my brother, but that was hardly noticeable as our schedules kept us from basically ever seeing each other. He was constantly working, and I was always in school and working as well. It was so strange feeling so alone in a home where you technically weren't. It was as if, while I was here, my head and heart were somewhere else. My mind was in the world I grew up in, the place I called home, and I was now stuck trying to understand this strange land I had entered.

Though my mother was not there to create delicious "caldos" on Sunday mornings that emitted a scent strong enough to pull any night owl out of bed, I quickly had to adapt to my new home in order to succeed and fulfill my purpose. I quickly began to view America, not as a foreign country, but more as a new beginning—as a land of fruitfulness, the kind that allowed me to hand over my check every week to my older brother in order to send it to my needy mother. The kind of land that gave me the opportunity to find who I was.

This process most definitely did not come in a symmetrical box adorned with ribbons and bows gently placed in my hands.

It took a lot of failure and reflection getting to know my limits and then pushing past them along with upholding my values and morals that have whole-heartedly affected the turnout of my life.

Whether it be waiting for my now wife to finish her education as an accountant before we got married so that we could have a solid foundation to grow from, to the immense feeling of pride as I entered different job situations in which I found myself able to perform the tasks of five men.

None of this is said in a sense of cockiness but in a sense of pride as in: "Wow, I'm actually doing it. I'm useful and able to contribute not only to my success but to this new country which I call home."

That to me was one of the biggest payoffs because I think with any new venture there always comes this fear of failing. Failing at the unknown, risking everything and being able to produce the outcome that compensates for all the struggle you have not only endured, but also the silent pain inflicted upon your loved ones and those around you.

The only way I was able to overcome that fear was through the word of God which eventually illuminated me with a realization—the realization that each and every one of us has an innate purpose that we were meant to share with the world and that some of us were granted several gifts, but don't realize that that gift is meant to be temporarily shared or that it does not fully encompass God's plan for you. Just how my career in Mexico did not last long, it was still a passion I kept alive as a struggling young boy gambling with quarters in order to go out and dance and let's not forget the endless invites to weddings and Quinceañeras. See, it is not necessary to kill all your dreams, but it is always important that even through failure, you continue to have ambition and aspirations to push you through life and to accept God's gift as your own.

Finally, that success shouldn't come at the cost of your freedom. That success should give you the freedom to enjoy your success. No one should be working like a mule in order to be happy. Now, being established as an eighteen-year business owner with a family to call my own, I've learned through being a father that one shouldn't work to the point of losing themselves. That even though my mother is no longer here with me, I carry her always and know she would be proud of what I've accomplished, that I know she wished she could've worked less and proved her love more. I also know that we never once doubted the love she had for us.

If I am to leave anything worth knowing on this earth, it is to give love. Being greedy is for the weak because it is through sharing and kindness that we make someone stronger, and at the end of the day, it is your acts that determine the people you attract into your life.

So, be generous and keep good company because when your knees become weak and you start to fall, the ones who are going to help you are whoever stands at your side.

CHICKEN FAJITAS

By Amador Jiménez

Fajitas

4 tablespoons canola oil, divided
2 tablespoons lemon juice
1 1/2 teaspoon of seasoned salt
1 1/2 teaspoon dried oregano
1 1/2 teaspoon cumin
1 teaspoon of garlic powder
1/2 teaspoon chili powder
1/2 teaspoon of paprika
1/2 teaspoon of crushed red pepper flakes, optional
1 1/2-pound boneless skinless chicken breast, cut into thin strips
1/2 medium sweet red pepper, julienned
4 green onions, thinly sliced
1/2 cup chopped onion
6 flour tortillas

1. Season meat with salt, oregano, ground cumin, garlic powder, chili powder, paprika, crushed red pepper (optional)

2. On a hot griddle, put oil and add your seasoned meat, and cook it down to ¾

3. Start putting the ingredients in this order: onion, peppers and finally the tomato.

4. Squeeze the lemon.

5. When the vegetables are tender and the meat is cooked, put out the fire and serve on the previously heated tortillas.

CHEF AMBROCIO GONZÁLEZ

La Catedral Cafe y Las Quecas

6
Faith

"Ambrocio, what is your hurry in leaving?! There's no need to go . . . you have your job here . . . we're getting situated just fine. Don't go."

My mom shook her head as she began to marinate the meat in preparation for her famous typical Guadalajara dish "carne en su jugo." Our family is not into moving, so it's no surprise that when I presented her with the idea of going to the United States, her mentality didn't exactly match mine. The thing was that I had already thought about it. I thought about a life of just living paycheck to paycheck and working until the physical demand was just too much . I saw all of that in my mother, and I couldn't live

71

knowing there was something so much better waiting for us across that long pile of dirt. To be honest, at the very least, not giving into the possibility of alleviating my mother's stress in any way felt as if I was robbing a bit of purpose from her life each day.

"Mom, you know why. I don't make enough money with my job here, not even close to what I could be making in the U.S. Just imagine the possibilities and all the things we'll be able to have with that money. I'll be fine. I won't be long either—just enough time to save up what Tio makes, and before you know it, I'll be back. Nice and simple."

I tried to flash a reassuring smile in my mom's direction, but I guess she knew better than I did that the journey was not as easy as I was making it seem.

"Mijo, it's not that easy. Haven't you seen the movies?!"

Of course, I can't help but chuckle to myself a tad remembering how my mom watched all of the newscasts and famous movies depicting the long and treacherous journey across the desert that many before me had taken and of the inhumane scenes of new immigrants being chased down by police. All in all, there was no escaping the melancholic tone my news had brought into the room, but I think after some time, my mom realized that there was also no way of escaping the fact that I had made up my mind, and that I really was leaving.

A few days later, I went to the Corona factory, where I was working at the time, and also shared with them the new trek I had in mind. Ideally, I would've kept my job in Mexico on hold, like most students do. They get a job, return to school for the time being, but upon arrival back home, their post is there happy and waiting for them with arms wide open. The only thing is that my job wasn't as willing as I might have thought. When I presented them with the news, they questioned me, and asked me if I was sure (which is funny because it seems that when you present most people with some sort of change, they always ask that question. "Are you sure?" As if their passive concern might inflict a change of heart on your behalf or as if you might have bumped your head and are now walking around with delirious thoughts).

After the initial shock, they basically told me that they couldn't promise my position because even after I had told them I was only due to stay for about a year in the U.S., they corrected me by saying, "If you're going, you're not coming back . . ."

I don't think either of us truly digested the truth that casual prediction would have in the future.

Upon my resignation, I was also forced to sign a contract that stated that I would no longer be able to work at any of the other beer companies they had. It took a lot for me to sign that sheet considering it was the one true job that really held promise for me at the time, but I figured it was just another sacrifice I would have to take in order to attain the future I wanted.

I did, for a moment—right before I put the tip of the pen to paper, think about everything that had led up to that moment . . .

I thought about my mother converting her nursing shifts at her hospital into makeshift daycares and how the small areas were my well-known playrooms, and I know to some that may seem upsetting, but on the bright side, at least they were sterilized.

If anything, the conditions at the hospital boosted my creativity levels. Do you know how challenging it is to play story time with a pair of medical gloves and some syringes?

Sure, I accommodated myself, especially my little area under one of the tables in a nearby room. Most days, though, I would cry as even the fluorescent ceiling lights' warmth couldn't keep me company. Then, there was one day when my innocent heart just couldn't take it any longer, where the stainless-steel countertops just didn't cut it, and the darkness of the night sky seemed to reflect off the clean-cut white walls more than it usually did. On this day, along with my cries, I scuttled to the room's connected patio and let out some pretty concerning banshee shrieks. On this night, I didn't want to be the obedient kid who pretended to be okay with being tossed into an empty room no matter how much I knew it had to be done. I didn't want to be the kid who muffled his tears so nurses passing by couldn't hear and who seemed to be satisfied with some antibacterial hand spray for play. That day, I was the kid who missed his mom, who wanted to play, but most of all, that night I was the kid who wanted to be heard, and I can assure you that that is exactly what happened.

Some medical staff in the surgical department overheard the alarming screams and were quite confused by the origin of them, except for one person: my mother. She knew exactly where the "bloody Mary" cries were coming from.

Once my mother entered the room, she did something that surprised me. She wasn't mad at all. Instead, she ran to me and consumed me in her arms allowing all of her to enter me as a shield of safety. It was her way of soothing me and telling me that she understood my frustration and fear, that she was here, and in that moment, I realized that the only wish my mom had was to always just be here.

I thought of the beautiful vibrancy of my home and my grandfather who was the only father figure I had ever known. I also thought of our Christmases together and our tradition of setting up the annual nativity scene across the kitchen and how on one December fourteenth, when we began to set up it again, my grandpa wasn't there to help. Actually, I didn't know where my grandpa was at all until I heard a shrilling scream that sent a boulder down my stomach and an emptiness crawling within me. That night, the Christmas spirit died with my grandfather, the nativity scene's unfinished state reflected our energy to pursue anything, and for three years it stayed there as an adornment to remembering his life with us.

Yes, all these thoughts flew through my mind like the constantly changing scenes you pass as you drive along the highway.

Finally, I was brought back to the moment I was in contract in front of me, pen in hand. I thought of the amazing opportunity at this very company that I was standing at that day, willingly giving up every opportunity and option they had ever given me.

I thought of the trips and people I had gotten to know through this job, and I began to question whether I really knew what I was doing— whether I was truly ready to give all of this up. As I was traveling down memory lane, I couldn't help but remember in that exact moment when my life changed, when in a meeting full of people, the then CEO had asked me to stand up and ask me about my age . . .

"Hey kid! How old are you?!"

Then, suddenly, I wasn't in my mind any more, I was ankle deep in the Tucson Desert just a few days away from reaching that promised land I had left so much for. It was really through those days I began to feel humbled because in those situations one really is depending on the kindness of others for either food shelter or transportation.

But sometimes kindness was the last thing we encountered. Truly, some of these people I could not even imagine being humans. They would corral us in at the bottom of trucks to get us across. I'll never forget a family in Phoenix who had the audacity to correct our posture as we sat on the ground of their kitchen, starved for three days while they had a whole dinner in front of us, just mocking us at our disparity.

Through trial and tribulation, I kept surprising myself with how much I could take each day. Once I arrived in Chicago, the struggle continued as I arrived at the so-called lavish life my grandma had promised me.

See, the only reason my uncle was receiving such a high wage was because he was a chauffeur for a company he had already been with for a number of years. I, on the other hand, had no sort of relationship. I spent my time going to work agencies day after day, searching and getting new jobs. Some were bad, and others were worse. I got stuck doing the jobs that nobody wanted, and let me tell you, they definitely did not pay the weekly $1,500 checks my grandma had promised.

It wasn't long before regret started to seep its way into my being, and it wasn't in a gentle progressive stream. It was hard and all at once, like the backhand of reality punishing me on my mother's behalf for even once thinking I was going to be granted a blissful journey, as if I was so special. I started a new life here, one that was constantly pulling out parts of me I didn't know existed in order to survive each day. This is where I truly felt like a "nobody," like a paper doll floating through the wind with no grasp on how to take hold of my reality. My significance was as disposable as an old, used Kleenex.

Those feelings don't just form on their own, and sometimes your strength can take much more than a quick jab from life, but it's the actions of those we encounter that have some inexplicable way of disturbing our original inner being.

See, the earth makes its rotation around the sun, and through this, we are here living and breathing all the changes it offers us.

Some things are beautiful like the vibrant colors of a blossoming tulip yearning for your hands to graze upon its feeble petals or the refraction of sunlight against a clear lake imitating the dancing of midnight stars as if reminding you they were still there. On another hand, some are much colder, like breathing in air with tiny daggers to your throat inducing a cold that spreads well beneath your bones. Its so desperate that you learn to numb out the pain as you work on the outside of a house so that a family of strangers you'll never meet can stay warm while your right hand may have frostbite.

But who knows you're numb? No one.

As an agency worker, we were provided with special commodities besides "new and exciting" tasks every day. They also provided us with our own personal chauffeur to take us to and from our job and the agency every day. No exceptions . . . you go to your job and the agency every day.

"No exceptions," he said, "I take you to your job, and then to the agency every day. Today is no different. You can go home from there."

This was when chills begin to run through my spine as the foggy view of my street corner begins to dissipate a little more as we drove by it. It was the middle of winter, and I had just finished a grueling day of work with snow to my knees and the warmth of my body slowly extinguishing. Of course, with the perks of a chauffeur, who needed a car? Especially when you can't afford one. With no way of getting home past this cold, I quickly asked the driver to please let me off on the corner by my house. It was the street we were already on, and the last thing I wanted was to cause an inconvenience, which is what I believed I was avoiding.

Take a guess on what he responded...

...No.

We were pulling up into the agency. I looked down at my second hand, hand-me-down, thrift-shop, permeable "work" shoes; they looked like there were a thousand places they'd rather be than trudging through inches of snow, and I was right there with them. That day I walked twenty blocks just to get home. I went through twenty blocks of ice water in my socks. Twenty blocks of "come on we're almost there" chants in my head. Twenty blocks of blowing whatever heat I could ignite into my hands that now really were numb. Twenty blocks of asking God, "What have I done?!" Twenty blocks of the oxygen punishing my lungs with stinging embraces. Twenty blocks of realizing snowflakes aren't as beautiful as people make them out to be when their cold touch covers your face like mask.

I got home, and wasn't sure if I was even capable of producing tears, but the act was there, and you can believe that I was trying. I had reached a point where there was just not enough ignition in my drive; I was completely exhausted. My grandmother was there watching as I changed out of my drenched clothing and I could tell it hurt her to see me, but I couldn't help but feel anger even toward her for selling me a false dream, and then even more anger toward myself for being so naive as to leave everything behind and follow that dream. I contemplated many things, like going home. My mom was always telling me everything would be different there, that we may not have much but it would be enough.

It's just that "enough" wasn't enough for me. I knew that I was meant to come here for a reason, that everything that's happened to me has happened because of something, and that I wasn't done with my journey just yet.

My grandmother knew about the urge I had to have my own restaurant— that I just kept having an itch to be my own boss and run a place I could call mine. I couldn't just stay in a day-to-day job situation forever.

A lot of things happened when that man left me out in the cold. They're very little things, but they change your mentality. At times, you can feel just enough suffering to push you over the edge because people will go on living their lives with no real understanding of what they've caused you.

You may not remember me, but there's a chilliness to your face *I could never forget.* I know you don't remember me. Why would you? You're so quick to dump things, to forget. You have probably so easily dumped me from your memory. You may not recall, Sir, but you have no idea what you have caused me...

In my head, time froze, and I think I might've stared for a little too long, but all in all the interaction took a total of maybe three seconds. On a day like any other, while walking to work I saw him; it was he who gave no thought to my well-being as he willingly sacrificed me to the open tundra. It may sound a little melodramatic, but that's how it felt. And it takes time to thaw from those experiences because, try as I might, even with the goal of being as kind as I can be, you can't always stop the cold from entering parts of your heart.

I finally reach the steps to La Catedral, in other words, blood, sweat, and tears constructed into a restaurant. It's early morning, and I'm bringing in new produce for the day. I put the key in, twisting the doorknob open along with the clinking music of neighboring keys around a metal ring, and I admire the vacancy inside, the emptiness of its existence, a raw skeleton waiting to fill with the life of the bustling lunch rush. As I set my bags down, I look out the window to see young people running along on the sidewalk, their infectious laughter spreading through my walls filling La Catedral with their young spirit.

I remember the struggle I put into this place, the nights of turmoil of not eating, of not living—for a dream I knew I had to realize. I remember the constant fight of having to make one more dollar than the last because that's the measly life I was living. I stand here, today, in the vacant skeletal form of everything that wasn't supposed to happen, and I smile, thanking God a million and three times more than I did when I arrived safely to an adventure I now know I was ready for. I sit here and quickly remember that it's Sunday, and the lines will be out the door, so nostalgia can't stay for too long. In its place sits the relevance of faith and humility.

Yes, faith and humility. Against the silence of the dawn, they whisper: *Don't stop believing . . .*

TORTA AHOGADA

By Ambrocio González

Torta Ahogada

8 salted bread rolls
Stewed beans
2 pounds of chopped carnitas

Ingredients for onions
1 sliced onion
Oregano
Lemons
Salt and pepper to taste

Ingredients for tomato sauce
3 pounds of tomato
2 cups water
Chopped half an onion
1 pinch of cumin and clove
1/2 teaspoon oregano
2 cloves garlic
Salt to taste

Ingredients for Spicy Sauce
50 grams of Chile de Arbol
1 cup of water
2 cloves garlic
Half a cup of white vinegar
Salt to taste
Pepper to taste

For salsa
1. Boil the tomato and then blend it with water, chopped onion, garlic cloves, cumin, clove and salt to your liking. If it becomes too thick, add a little more water.

2. Season the sauce in a frying pan with a little oil and add the teaspoon

of oregano, crumble the oregano in your hands to make sure it is well ground.

For the hot sauce
Cook the peppers in water, then blend with one cup of water garlic, pepper, vinegar and salt to taste.

For onions
Put the sliced onion in a container. We put the juice of three lemons, a little salt, pepper and oregano to taste.

To prepare the cakes
Open the rolls in half, spread the refried beans, add the meat and immerse them in a dish filled with the tomato sauce. Add hot sauce to taste.

Add some onions with lemon and get ready to enjoy the exquisite Torta Ahogada

CHEF ENRIQUE CORTÉZ

—

7
Discipline

Cooking is life to me. It's a way of maintaining my sanity behind all the chaos of the world. It's, in a sense, my own dosage of freedom as I embark upon the endless days of life.

Even my perception of life experiences has been adjusted because of this. I experience everything through my senses: events, shows, meetings. It's all a story that has slowly been engrained within each atom of sensory perception inside me. At times, I can look at a mixture of a dish, witness the texture, analyze the different flavor combinations, and simply—with that look—create my own mental combinations and judge the possible outcome from there.

Growing up in Sonora, Mexico, came with the most unconventional food combinations one could imagine. It was a mass array of typical Mexican dishes mixed with those unlike anything any of the other states had to offer. We made food out of everything, putting melon into soup the way my grandmother used to make and had different racial groups incorporate their own culture and flavor into our traditional cuisine.

I grew up in a huge household of about seven siblings. To this day, I cannot even fathom how my mother handled it. Sometimes I cannot even handle my two kids. My older siblings were born in the D.F. of Mexico (Mexico City) and therefore experienced a different world than I did with a different palate for life. After months of my aunts begging my mom to move to California, she finally began to consider the options of living closer to family and figured if they have their own homes and portray such a happy lifestyle, why can't we too?

We finally moved, and let me tell you, it was different. It wasn't like living in a state because you're cut at this weird intersection of both countries and nothingness. The nothingness spawned from the huge majority of desert that was available for viewing, biking or just day-to-day escape.

By the time we moved, I was four or five and saw life with a new perspective, especially given the fact that some of the population of Sonora is Asian. I know it's the oddest thing when you run into a stranger with the name "Luis Chen."

These Asian people with pale skin and delicate features are full-fledged Mexicans who eat tacos and speak just like us but have ancestors from their fathers or grandfathers who gave them their unique look. And many tend to continue to offer their unique taste of life for us as well but with a delicious fusion of their past and present identity.

I hold a great tie to this food and culture because they are some of the only things that bring me back to my brother, a brother who was lost much too soon and whom I feel I am deeply connected to.

I don't think I can forget the day the tragedy, that would ultimately help define me, happened because it was almost as if my brother was calling for me in that moment. I remember waking up in the middle of night in sweats and breathing so heavily that it felt as if my diaphragm was being held hostage behind the hard cage of my ribs and was just itching for a way out. It was four in the morning, and I wasn't sure what was wrong, but I knew that something was off in the atmosphere.

In that moment, one of my younger siblings slammed my door open and told me that my older brother had been in a tragic car accident. In that moment, I knew what the inevitable truth would soon bring; I knew that he was gone. It was hardest given the fact that I was very close to my sister-in-law. One day, as I was driving home, I felt this energy within me and a presence in my car. I wasn't scared. I didn't even flinch because I knew my brother was right there with me protecting every step I decided to take. Just like when he guided and convinced me to make the journey to the United States—a decision that I was so unsure of. See, I was studying gastronomy in Michoacán, and at that moment, I felt like I was a kid in Disneyland with all the freedom and grace in the world, but I knew there was no future for me here.

A majority of time, I feel as if young people, especially in their early twenties, are looking for some type of support or recognition and often it's not from their families or friends that they seek it, it's from their careers or what their interests are. It's quite an easy concept; people want to feel that they're good at something. To receive some sort of confirmation that their passion isn't a waste. I knew that that was something I wasn't going to discover where I was. I knew that even though I loved the diversity I experienced in my town, it just wasn't the place for me to receive anything that I needed. That, and also living right by the border, came with an inevitable possibility that I was going to eventually cross to the U.S.

Now, as I reflect on my life and the deeds that I've been able to accomplish, I recognize it was all because of the inner values my family had set on me. I was always disciplined as a child so that if I said that I was going to do something, it was going to be done.

I know that when you think of discipline it usually comes with negative thoughts of no freedom and controlling authoritarian behavior, but I think that that is often a huge misconception. People don't often realize that there is no way for you to reach your goals in life if you don't have some set plan and have the will, drive, discipline and strength to accept the struggle that comes with the journey and to follow it without question.

Discipline doesn't always mean a monotonous routine of life but a strong mindset that isn't easily swayed by life's disappointments and temptations. It's the ability to say "Yes, I can do this" and "I will do this because I will not be the one to stop myself."

The last thing I wish to say is to not give up because the universe has a funny way of always making things happen. Now, whether they happen at the time that you want them to is a different issue, but I promise your life has a way of giving you everything you need—not at the time that you want it or the time you think you need it—but at the time that life knows you need it.

PAELLA VEGETARIANA
By Enrique Cortéz

Paella Vegetariana
Serves Two

1 onion, chopped
2 garlic cloves, chopped
1 red bell pepper
1 green bell pepper
½ cup finely chopped parsley
1 ½ cups cremini mushroom
12 threads of saffron
1 ½ cups of paella rice (Arborio or Spanish bomba)
3 ½ cups of vegetable stock with a dash of turmeric
1 cup of peas
3 tbsp. olive oil
1 zucchini (Julianne)
1 artichoke, cut in small pieces
salt, pepper, and lemon for taste

1. Heat the oil in a wide casserole dish.
2. Add onions and garlic, and sauté until slightly golden.
3. Add the rice and vegetables, stir for three minutes.
4. Add seasonings and stock, bring to a boil.
5. Cover and cook over low heat for 20-30 minutes.

For our **Paella La Taberna** (with seafood, chicken, pork, chorizo) add 4 mussels, 6 shrimps, 2 sliced squids, small pieces of chicken, pork, and Spanish sausage.

Garnish with parsley, fresh red and green bell peppers, and slices of lemon.

ANGELA LAVELLI
Café La Fortuna

—

8
Love

There are times when the breeze hits me just right and the sun positions itself as if it were slightly peeking out just to see my eyes. And then, there's something in that moment that leaves me confused on which land my feet walk upon. One part of me is moved by the smells from puffs of flour taking over the air, and I feel the Tuscan sunset lay upon my shoulders, while another part of me hears the chorus of laughter in my grandparents' Mexican home accompanied by the explosion of seasonings in our family meal. After a few moments of this nostalgia, I open my eyes and realize these places are only parts that lay within me, none of which I can call home.

I drop my daughter off to school and head to work at our family-owned café that has provided so much for us and has enabled us to call this land, America, our home.

It must be that my father's unexpected move to Mexico from Italy set the foundation for change and migration in my genes, and that has sent me to places I never imagined.

When I was young, I have memories of having play dates with my brother and a group of thirty-year-old Italians that were either our family or extended family. Well, honestly, in Italy, anyone who walks through your front door ends up being family, so we had a big one. We were two Mexican kids from Mexico City: no friends, no toys, no television, attempting to entertain ourselves in a country that was my father's, a little bit of my own, but where was really overall unknown.

As the summers in Italy grew more frequent, our brains started subtly picking up the vocabulary and the emotion around us, slowly transitioning us into an Italian state of mind. I never picked up a book, never took a course on how to speak Italian; my brain just understood it. That, in a sense, helped fill some of the time while we sat around our uncles and aunts and listened to the daily news in town. When we weren't slightly eaves dropping into the conversations, my brother and I would become very creative with the world around us, creating games out of rocks and sticks, people watching... Now that I think about it, I'm very glad that I had my brother with me on those trips. He was my own personal sidekick in this little adventure of ours.

There was one thing, though, that was both our favorite in Italy and Mexico and wherever we went. We had a routine where we would attempt to stuff our faces with breakfast as fast as we could in order to make it to the fresh daily market every single day. That's one custom that I've learned to love especially from the European culture. We never filled our refrigerators to the top or had a pantry that was ready to bust. The real excitement was going to the markets and smelling the basil freshly picked, its aroma slowly taking over our senses. The adrenaline came from getting to choose what we were going to eat that day in that instant then bringing it home and knowing that you could do it all again the very next day.

I'm not sure what it is about it, but there's something in the atmosphere during that time that poured glee into my body. Thinking back on it, those moments were probably the ones that set my love and passion for cooking from the start.

Being in the kitchen for me is something that not only makes me happy but alleviates the stress of my daily life; it puts me at peace. I think that has to do with food not only containing ingredients, but rather requesting an investment from you physically and spiritually.

Our food will speak on behalf of its creator. In other words, if you're happy and excited to be preparing your meal, and you're cooking it with love and passion, then your food will emit that, but if you're cooking with a bitter feeling, then you better believe that everyone will be able to taste that in your dish.

With that theory in mind, I guess that's why my father's dishes were the best. Well, they weren't really just my father's, they were ours because those dishes were full of laughter and beautiful moments. For example, our favorite was cooking homemade ravioli, and when I mean *homemade*, I mean completely *homemade* from scratch—from the dough to the sauce to creating its shape—everything was made by hand. It was a miracle that we even ended up with anything to eat considering the fact that half of our batch was eaten raw. The other half was considered the survivor that actually got to be cooked and served.

It was a beautiful process that, in the end, served not only our stomachs but our hearts as it was a meal shared as a family. Aunts, uncles, cousins, and siblings would all sit around the table or even on the floor just reminiscing on the days past. And even though it took a lot of time, I remember my father's Italian voice telling me, "*Chi va piano va lontano*" which basically means, "That who goes slowly goes far." It was a way of reminding us to enjoy life piece by piece, not rushing through it, because I feel as though there are many times when as you try to rush through things and you become less attentive towards them instead of really focusing and enjoying the ride as it comes.

Fast forwarding some years, I went to university, following in my mother's footsteps and studying accountancy. There, I met my husband and started to really begin what would be the rest of my life. Once I graduated college, my husband and I were still together and attempting to find out how we were going to obtain financial stability when we really had none. Now, my husband grew up working his whole life. His family had a house in the state of Chiapas which . . . let's just say...was not my favorite. The weather is too hot.

I was a young driven accountant who was working an office job, a wife, and a lost soul looking to find a place to call home. I remember my husband telling me, "Well if we can't find a place and we're not economically able to, then we're going to end up living in that plantation whether you like it or not." I didn't know how we were going to do it, but there's one thing you must know about me and that is that I do not do spiders or bugs or anything that crawls in any way. So for me that news basically broke down my vision of a dream home—but not all hope was lost. Soon, we heard news of a local selling an open space where their business used to be along with coffee equipment, and this wasn't a regular everyday coffee maker in someone's home. This was the kind that would roast and a grind up the beans making actual real coffee for many people. Since my husband was the only one with experience in this, he jumped at the idea to open a coffee shop. Quite honestly, I wasn't really opposed to the idea. I was actually excited that this was going to be our first big adventure together, and I was happy to do it with him. So, that's what we did. We started being able to provide for ourselves with our new business. Everything was going alright, but sometimes life really is too good to be true, and quickly my tables were turned.

Once I graduated from the university and obtained my degree in accountancy, my father and brother had an idea of opening a restaurant, an idea I completely supported but one which I really had no business in. No, I was definitely more of a sideline cheerleader.

The construct of our family was good. My mother was working as an accountant, my father and brother were running the restaurant, and my husband and I were busy with our children and running our own café. However, there was something that continuously went around while all of this was occurring. At this point, obviously, my sibling and I were grown. We were beginning our own lives, and along with that growth day by day my parents matured as well. Now my dad was doing all right. He clearly was still working with my brother, but he suddenly became very ill, having a heart attack that would send him to the hospital. There was always that bit of fear of going to the hospital and spending a few days there. This time, though, there was no happy ending, and he didn't come out. I couldn't really describe to you what it feels to lose someone like that because it wasn't just my father that slipped away from me, it was my world.

My father was everything I was because you must remember that that ravioli wasn't just pasta, it was laughter and love; it was the beginning of the creation of who I am today, and it's hard to just accept that it's all gone.

It's as if the air that you breathed every day was bottled up and thrown into a faraway abyss because suddenly that air wasn't yours anymore. It was a devastating moment for all of us, but I knew that I had to help carry on his name in whatever way that I could. So, I joined my brother in the restaurant that he had previously owned with my father so as to help him as much as I could, even though it was never a part of my plan. As the years went by, I would teeter totter between my café and my brother's restaurant. It was a load, but I was always taught to value the meaning of family no matter what hardships they bring.

Eventually, though, I had to leave the restaurant. At that point, it just became too much to be directing our café, being a mother, being a wife and then still having to work at my brother's restaurant. Even though it was a tough decision, I think we all knew it was the right one for me and for our family overall.

The moments of bliss continued and then they were stolen . . . no, they were literally stolen. Let me explain to you the turning point in my life. It's not that complicated but rather quite simple actually. One day, my children and I went out. My husband was at work. My children and I got home at the end of our night, and there was something off. When I walked into my bedroom the necklace that my father made me the day of my wedding, my children's passports, our visas, you guessed it, gone. Things, so familiar and treasured, gone. My house was turned upside down. This day, ladies and gentlemen, began a very long journey of suffering and constant paranoia.

One would think that they would be able to call the police, get some DNA, find the culprit, and call it a day, but that is far from what happened. The police, after many days of searching and ending up with nothing, told us there wasn't enough substantial evidence to make any case, and here's the funny part: by this point, my husband and I took the liberty of doing our own investigation. We found our own clue sleuthing around, and summed up a rather valid guess on a potential suspect. We found out it was somebody we knew, someone close to us, who—as much as we wanted to lay the hand of the law on them—the law was rather picky that day and decided that our pieces of evidence were not enough. Since they couldn't find anything, in their opinion, our case was closed, dismissed, and our theft accepted.

This is what I want people to understand about a home burglary, it's not the physical things that they take from you. It's what keeps you up at night, the peacefulness of sleep that is truly stolen. It's the fact that I didn't feel comfortable in my own home. Like those scenes from children's cartoons when the character walks by a painting in the hall, and its eyes are still moving with you. It's just like that but in real life. You know no one is there, but you can't help but think that maybe he is. As if every corner has eyes and every window is being used as a magnifying glass to see you. An inevitable feeling conjures as you begin to create nonsensical situations as if everyone is out to get you, in such a way that every possession of yours is of interest. It begins to suffocate you.

I remember that I would shut my windows and sleep with my door locked and still feel at risk, and as much as I tried, I could not get over this feeling—to the point that I told my husband I couldn't take it anymore. We had to go. I didn't mean just move homes. My leap needed to be much bigger than that.

The fact was that I didn't feel safe in my own country, my Mexico.

That's how we moved to the United States with a little piece of hope because in all honesty, we weren't sure if we would be able to. We had a café still in Mexico and we decided to move to the United States arriving in Lombard, Illinois, about few miles west of Chicago—first with the hopes that because of my Italian ancestry we would be able to obtain residency.

With no promise that we would be able to stay, we figured that we would stay a few months, and if we could stay in the United States, then it was meant to be, and if not, we would just move back, but the last thing we wanted to do was to be running a business where every few days or so it would mean traveling back and forth between countries. Thankfully, all of that was avoided since we were granted our residency. I couldn't have been happier.

Yes, sometimes I miss home like anybody does because at the moment, my only family here was my husband and my children.

Sometimes I miss the street food in Mexico or the fresh markets I would go to, but I knew that if I wanted to be at peace, I would need to be here.

Even though we're settled now, it has taken us a long time to get where we are. We still have a café in Mexico which is being run by some amazing individuals who we basically call family. They oversee the direction and overall success of our café. People need to understand that in any type of business, but especially one where you're not constantly there, it's extremely hard to find people whom you trust will have the best interest for your business and that it comes from a genuine place. So, our family feels very lucky to have found that.

We also have our two businesses here, and we are still making coffee. Through a failed business and failed partnerships, we have learned and grown. One thing that hasn't failed, though, is the partnership between my husband and me. You would think spending twenty-four hours with the same person 365 days a year would eventually create some sort of conflict, but the best thing that I can say is that I fell in love with my best friend, and no amount of time could ever change that.

There will always be struggles, hardships, and sad moments especially being a whole country away from your homeland. Of course, there are times where I felt judged simply for being who I was or from where I am. Yes, there was a feeling of being incapable because I didn't speak the language adequately, but it doesn't take a specific language to become successful or, even more than that, to create an impact.

When you are to carry anything with you, let it be this: let it be tenacity, a constant striving toward honesty, and above all an unforgettable feeling of love toward your country. Remember to live life slowly. You will not believe how far it takes you.

TAMALES CHIAPANECOS
By Angela Lavelli

Makes 20 3" tamales

Preparation time: 120 minutes

Corn masa for tamales

2lbs. Of corn masa
1 lb. Pork lard
1 teaspoon salt
1 Pack of banana leaves cut into 8 "x8" squares

1. Put into mixer the corn masa with the pork lard and the salt.

2. Beat the masa until a small ball floats in a glass with water. Reserve

For the filling

½ lb. Pork, cooked and shredded
3 chicken breasts cooked and shredded
20 seedless prunes cut in half
20 olives cut in half
20 slices of roasted bell pepper
4 boiled eggs cut into 5 slices each

The Mole Sauce
3 large dried Ancho Chile
3 mulato Chiles
2 Pasilla peppers
4 tablespoons of pork lard
2 green tomatillos sliced in four
2 Roma tomatoes sliced in four
2 cloves garlic, sliced
1 sliced onion
2 oz. almonds

2 teaspoons of toasted sesame
½ teaspoon oregano
6 whole black peppers
1 cup chicken broth
1 teaspoon salt
1 chocolate tablet

1. Open the chiles and remove the seeds.

2. In a pan, put two teaspoons of pork lard and fry the chiles for 30 seconds.

3. Remove the chiles from the pan and put them in a container with 1 cup of water for 10 minutes, liquify and reserve in a container.

4. In the same pan, add two tablespoons of pork lard and fry the onion for 5 minutes, add the garlic, tomatillo and roma tomato and sauté for 10 to 15 minutes, then grind in the blender until finely ground, return to the pan and add the chilies.

5. In a processor, grind the almond with the sesame seeds (ajonjoli), oregano and the black peppers until they are finely chopped.

6. Add this mixture to the pan with the chiles, add the chocolate tablet and stir until dissolved, add the chicken stock and salt, cook for 10 minutes taking care that the sauce does not dry much, if necessary add the water required.

7. Cut the banana leaves into squares and put them to cook in a pot with boiling water for about 20 minutes, being careful not to break them.
8. Strain the water well. Use the warm leaves to join the tamales.

9. Blend a 1/3 cup of the tamale dough in the center of the banana leaf, leaving 1 "on the edge. Put a piece of mole on the dough and put a piece of pork, a piece of chicken, a prune, a slice of red chile morron, an olive and a slice of egg.

10. Close the tamale along the filling as if it were an envelope, then fold the ends into a square. Use cooking wire to close the tamales or

banana leaf wires.

11. Cover the bottom of a steamer with the banana leaves and place the tamales.

12. Cook for 45 minutes or until the tamale easily detaches from the banana leaf.

To serve, remove the tamale from the banana leaf and serve it with beans and cream.

ROBERTO CARLOS ÁVILA

Altiro Latin Fusion Restaurant

———

9
Trust

There are some things that you just don't see anymore, you know what I'm talking about? Like, those posts that you see on Facebook or social media, the ones that go . . . *If you didn't do this, you didn't experience a childhood.*

Well, I am happy to say that I was very fortunate to have experienced a childhood, where the streets and alleys weren't just for walking or for cars to pass by, but were a makeshift World Cup center where you would practice to become the next soccer star or where you could learn how to run pretty fast after you shot a ball toward a neighbor's window. Most of all, they were the best of times because we spent them playing amongst the dirt and dust, meeting kids from all over the block who would instantly join in on games and quickly becoming best friends. Whether it was by myself or among others, there's no denying that I truly experienced a wonderful childhood.

It's important to note though that being a kid doesn't always mean just fun and games. There comes a time where that part of you is set aside because real life is inevitable, and it comes sweeping in full throttle with no one to stop it. In my household, I was among the youngest of three brothers and a sister. Now, imagine this—it wasn't just a household of young kids because we weren't necessarily that far off in age, it was an apartment of kids where it seemed like we were moments from busting at the seams.

The apartment probably aided in forcing us to become close as a family by actively propelling us into one anothers lives. It was always very important to my father that we were ready for life and knew how to tackle it head on. His favorite thing to tell us was, "In order to be a good parent, you need to be a good teacher." This is a saying that has resonated with me ever since because in every aspect of its meaning, it's true.

My father had his business, but I still had a job of my own. I would still go out and pick up extra jobs like painting or setting down floors— really, whatever we found—but through this job, I found that wherever it is that you want to go, it's necessary that you build yourself from the bottom up.

If you want to be the boss and take charge of your life, you need to know how to do a peasant's job because it is only then that you will be able to ask someone else to do something for you.

Even though there are times you need help as a leader, you still need to establish those foundations for yourself, so you know that the work that is being done is done right and to assure that you're not being taken advantage of.

So, even though I was the son of the owner, I didn't get any lavish treatment nor were my mistakes greeted with a blind eye. If anything, I received even more scrutiny than any other employee, and that's not said in annoyance, but rather in pride because I know that every day that I spent working has built the character of who I am today. I wasn't just tied to our family business either. Our work went from setting floors, painting homes, and even cleaning walls—basically anything we could do to bring in a little extra cash. It's something that at the time and as a child, you don't always understand fully, but what my father was trying to instill in us is something so special that I would never want to grow up any other way.

He established the importance of being as knowledgeable as possible in as many things as you could so that when the time came, we wouldn't be blindly trusting others to help us because we now knew things of our own and knew when a job was well done.

Now, I don't want to paint the story as if working was the only thing that occupied my timeframe because let's not forget that childhood, mentioned earlier. You may be confused, asking yourself, "But Ricardo how did you have such a great childhood when you spent so much of it working?" Well, here's the catch, you learn to enjoy the life you've been given because it's the only one you've got.

Now, I may not have been the most liked child in the neighborhood, but I would argue that I was the one who had the most fun. I would spend every moment I could making dirt piles fly, reenacting the winning kick to finally end the game. I remember long afternoons playing in alleys or any open areas I could find, kicking a soccer ball around on my own or accompanied by other schoolmates. The rush of making passes or the celebratory adrenaline rush of a winning goal was so addictive that if I would've continued for any longer, I wouldn't be here telling you this story. I think that if things would've played out any other way, I might've been on one of your children's jerseys or somewhere making Coke commercials or headlining huge soccer matches, but after a visit to the States with my wife and kids, that all changed.

It was as if something changed in my wife's mind as she nonchalantly said to me," You know, honey, why don't we move here?" By that time, I really didn't have a response. I mean, why shouldn't we? We were reaching hard times in Mexico, where life wasn't anything to be envious about. The peso was dropping, and I had to start working as a taxi driver even on special holidays to keep my family afloat. There wasn't anything particular that was holding me back. With that, our minds were made up, and our voyage began.

I'm not coming to you with the typical story of travel and struggle because, really, getting here wasn't that hard, but there are a lot of stories that do start off that way. The beginning is blissful until you start realizing you're not really sure what you've gotten yourself into. I started realizing little things that maybe didn't quite faze me then but were hitting me smack dab in the face with a poster labeled, "reality." I realized I didn't know how to speak the language here, and that little detail would be fine if it wasn't so important to communicate. I started to realize that maybe this journey was not going to be as easy as expected.

As soon as my wife and I arrived, we started working in restaurants right away. We spent about seven to eight years working through the ranks of the kitchen. I started off as a dishwasher, cook, busboy, and waiter before I put a sudden stop to my restaurant employee career.

There was a certain thing that always occurred to me. I always seemed to be very well-liked by my superiors, and that's not said in arrogance at all. It's just a simple fact, and the only reason this was is because I came to work with a purpose in mind. Every day I set the goal to be better than the man I was yesterday, to be one step closer to my overall goal. I knew what needed to be done, and I came in with the mentality and work ethic to get it done. It's because of this that my bosses kept promoting me as my time there passed, but suddenly when the position of manager opened up, my heart wasn't in it anymore. It's not that I no longer loved working with food, but more that I no longer wanted to work under the hand of somebody else. I figured that it had been too long; I knew I had the capabilities to do it, so why didn't I?

With that, I bid farewell to my old jobs, thankful for each one as they acted as fundamental strands weaving me into completion, enhancing my overall strength as a person, giving me the confidence to know when it was time to walk away. And when my bosses asked me to come back, it was only when I told them, "The only way I'm working in your kitchen again is if you make me a partner," that they understood the determination that had overcome me.

As time went by, the Lord and our faith manifested into the businesses we have today. Although it seems like a happy ending— which in a way it is—it holds some very hard moments. My wife's family has always been a huge anchor for me even when I decided to open my first restaurant. Her brothers became partners with us, and her mother was one of our biggest motivators. So in a sense, this restaurant isn't just mine, it's a representation of all of us, and above all it's a gift from God. So, when the Lord decided to take some of those people from that dream, well, it wasn't taken easily. First, it was my wife's brother who was a huge contributor to the restaurant. That was an enormous heartbreak that shook up our whole world. When her brother died—before the opening of the restaurant—we took the hit hard. We basically put out life on pause flying out to Mexico, financially and emotionally contributing as much as we could, and though moments like these never truly pass, we had to return to our lives. We recognized that now the journey would be a little harder. One thing that was special was when my mother-in-law took my wife and whispered to her these words, "If I die before this restaurant is open I don't want you to do what you did with your brother. I don't want you to come. I want you to stay here and be happy. I want you to continue your dreams and never let them go because I know you can do it."

The day we decided to open our doors with my wife by my side and children ready to help, I couldn't help but be overcome with a million emotions. I began to question whether I should pursue my dream, if it was worth it, even plausible, whether I was capable of such a thing. But before I let those thoughts taint my mind, I said a little prayer underneath my breath, and I thanked God for the fortune I had thus far. I didn't ask of Him anything that wasn't His will for me. I began to remember sitting by myself in the corner as I constructed the menu for our restaurant, asking to let His words and food be transmitted through my hands. I knew that everything here was His, and I was just here to share it. I opened my eyes and knew that God was with us and that there's no sense in trying to control things that have already been planned for you. So, I took an exhale and trusted in him.

That whole day, as my family and I were running around beginning what would soon be the epicenter of our lives, we didn't realize we had someone rooting for us, better yet breathing, living for us. My mother-in-law that day began dying slowly, her muscles and body began to shut down starting early on, working their way up to her heart. She laid there quietly not complaining of anything, started saying her subtle goodbyes and just waited. She waited there as the oxygen slowly became harder and harder to inhale, but she refused to die without one thing, and that was to hear my wife say that everything went great, and it seemed that everything was going to be okay with the restaurant.

At the end of the day, once we had finished up, my wife finally called her. The fatigue was clear in her voice, but it wasn't enough to trump the joy that was showering over us. I remember watching my wife smile and laugh with her, talk about everyday things, and it was when she finally told her about her day that the biggest sound of relief resonated between both of them. It was then that my mother-in-law stopped fighting because there was no longer anything to fight for. Her life was complete. She knew she was leaving her children okay and that her moment had come. With that, she let her last breath fall and silently slipped into peace.

The floor seemed to sink underneath my feet as the news of my wife's mother arose, and I didn't know what to do. I felt bad for feeling ecstatic to start the new day, yet felt terrible about her death. It was a whirlwind of emotions as it was, but you don't get to choose how your life plays out. You only get to choose your reaction to it. I offered to close the next day for my wife asking her if she was okay, but her response is one that will never fail to surprise me because it shows the commitment we both had for our future. "No, no I'll be fine, just give me an hour or so to cry, and I'll be fine," and that's exactly what she did. She took her time of mourning, and then jumped onto the restaurant floor with no hint of pain in her charming smile.

Though it seemed to be okay, of course doubts began to race through my mind, and I couldn't help but feel as though my mother-in-law's death was almost like an omen telling me that this was all just a bad idea, but in moments like those you begin to reflect on everything, and I remembered that my mother-in-law always pushed us to follow our dreams and do what felt right to us—that she made us promise that we would make this restaurant a reality. And with that, rather than falling to the feet of destiny, I continued my dream just as I believe she would've wanted.

Thankfully she was right, and I could not be more thankful for the cards life has dealt me. I have since opened more of my businesses expanding my passions which have enabled me to not only make this a business for me but for my family as well. Like my father, I try to instill the same values into my own children. The value of honesty and respect, of hard work and dedication—everything that has led me to my current place in life. These are values that I know have not been taken for granted because time and time again my children have shown me that they understand what it has cost us to get here. Whether it was when my daughter publicly spoke out on immigrant rights using my hard work as an example for others or my son's studies and hand-on help within the restaurant, this journey is not mine, but ours.

What the future holds only God and time will tell because life is not for the weak, and cowards don't last long, but as long as there's good company by my side and good food on my table I welcome it with open arms.

POLLO POBLANO

By Roberto Carlos

1 chicken breast
1/2 cup of flour
1 spoon Tera of Sazonador Italiano
 salt and pepper
1 lemon (juice)
1 spoon of tequila
chicken soup

Poblano cream
1 cup heavy cream
1 poblano pepper (peeled)
1/4 cup Chihuahua cheese
salt and pepper

Decor
pomegranate
cream

Preparation
1. In a very hot skillet put a little oil and the breasts with the flour and seasonings

2. Put the lemon juice and the tequila with the chicken broth to be reduced

3. Put in oven at 350⁰ until the chicken is finished for 8-10 min (check it out)

Cream
1. Put peeled poblano peppers in the blender with the heavy cream and cheese, salt and pepper

2. Once everything is blended, season in a pot with a little butter and do not stop moving until it takes a color and texture to taste.

3. Serve in a dish with poblano cream on top and pomegranate seeds to taste and with much love.

JUAN LUIS GONZÁLEZ

Mago Grill Restaurant

——

10
Family

There are really only two main ingredients to the recipe of life: a base of family, and mole . . . a whole lot of Grandma's mole to be exact.

Take note of that, it's very important.

It's way too easy to forget the true flavors of life and very hard to recover once they're gone.

As my journey in the United States continues, I find that preserving our roots is what enables each and every one of us to cultivate every ounce of potential we preserve.

Growing up in the state of Mexico with my family of eight has always been chaotic in a sense, but it always felt like home. I think that's one of the beauties of Mexico and of our culture—that we're all very family-oriented. It's knowing that seven other people are going to be accompanying me in this journey of life— individuals I will have ups and downs with—and, at the end of the day, knowing that I always have someone there for me and vice versa.

To me, this is a beautiful thing that not many people get. Family, above all else, is a strong principle that has always been evident in my life.

From a very young age, my family was always together living, learning and working.

I learned from those around me. Much of my father's family, my aunts and uncles and grandparents, had an amazing hand at cooking and probably since the age of five, my earliest memories are those of the kitchen.

I can remember helping with small things like cracking an egg here and there or stirring the pot while someone else was prepping the next dish. Every so often, I would help my grandmother who was always our designated chef whenever there were big events. In a flurry, the spices and flavors took over, and I believe that because I experienced this early in life, cooking took a hold of my heart and created in me a passion for it. Though it hasn't always been the road I believed I was destined to travel, it's the one that has always brought me back to home, and the one that, ultimately, I know was meant for me.

I was never big into TV or really any other things of that nature since I've always kind of liked being busy in that sense. So, when I wasn't in the kitchen, I was sent to help my dad with his work in whatever way I could. I will never forget my mother always ending her farewells or simply reminding us to work hard at whatever we do—that no matter if it was the most menial job, it should be done with effort and it should be done well.

At a very early age, I was always told to push on, and it was always something that was proven to me time and time again by example. In instances like my grandmother, who was a widow, I will forever admire her persistence and drive to push along my father and his siblings by herself. She worked and provided for them, gave them life, and all the necessities to survive and never asked for help. She refused to marry again because she just didn't see the point. She had gotten her children and her life this far along by herself, so she didn't see the point of adding someone else into the situation.

I firmly believe that if these hardships were to happen to anyone, they were meant to happen to my grandmother because out of everyone I know, she's the only one whose courage could've spanned that far and whose strength could've endured such pain.

When I wasn't going to school or working, the biggest event in our family was going to either lucha libre, bull fighting, or soccer. Now my dad was not a huge soccer fan . . . but lucha libre? Now, that's where everyone got immersed. My mother didn't share the same fondness toward the sport, but she willingly let us be consumed by the costumed men. Those were the best times for me. I became a fanatic of the sport, mesmerized by the reflection of light coming from the fighters' brightly colored shiny masks and watching how they skillfully faced their opponents like a well-choreographed dance. Each fighter's mind seemed focused slightly ahead of the next move, yet still depended on their teammates to guide them toward their next move. The hearty sound of men, women, and children each rooting for their guy in hopes of not losing all of that night's money on a silly bet made the environment so exhilarating that you could not even recall your decisions.

I remember my eyes widening as we would enter the arena, the excitement blazing across my pupils and the same look still being there by the end of the match. To me, there was no toy or movie that could beat that time I spent with my father.

Of course, days like that weren't always available as most of my time was spent working and going to school as a young boy. My father always believed education to be of the utmost importance. He always told us to continue studying, that that would be the biggest success we could receive. I, of course, silently nodded my head in agreement to an empty promise that I did not realize I was making. At the time, I had all the intentions of following my dad's wishes, and I myself believed that education was a step in my life that was clearly already set in stone.

As I got older, my mind began to shift, and suddenly it wasn't on the same page with what had already been mentioned. Suddenly, my father's ideas of me becoming an engineer not only became far-fetched, but undesirable. My life shifted and going to school just didn't seem to fit into where I wanted to go—which in this case wasn't even in this city . . . this state . . . shoot, not even this country.

I wanted to go to the United States. I'm not exactly sure where this desire came from, but I knew it was my next step, and, as I presumed, my father was not too thrilled about it. He, of course, questioned why I didn't want to pursue my education, giving me the all too familiar talk on how it was essential for me.

Now, this is not to say education is not essential because it is, but I was ready to make my own decisions, which my father would eventually just agree with and take this jump in my life.

Their worries and doubts came with good reason. Although it's not odd to see a young person like me, who was 22 at the time, have an exciting idea of what it is to venture into a new foreign country which you have no knowledge of and think that success is a platter served as the main entrée for dinner your first night.

That is the main issue for people who think that that is what coming to this country is, that it's a tough walk to get here but that once you arrive, money comes knocking at your door from one night to the other. That's just not the way it is.

I knew this, of course. I knew I was going to start from a very low position, and although I wasn't sure where I was headed, I knew that it was essential for me to start there. So at the age of 22, I packed my bags and came directly to Illinois, where I started working as a dishwasher in two different locations. One was a restaurant where I would work mornings and the second was a bakery where I would work afternoons and any other times I had off. The bakery holds a special place in my memory because it was the place that really gave me the push toward larger responsibilities that I wanted to have. I was the only Hispanic in that bakery, which was run by African Americans who didn't know a lick of Spanish, and I obviously couldn't rely on English. So, our relationship plodded along with some work. I will never forget when one of the workers there came up to me with a dictionary that translated English to Spanish and started attempting to communicate with me. He would write down his orders and any other messages he had, and at the same time I would begin learning the words as well. I began to get along very well with the guy. He would take me home after long days of work, and I started noticing that ever, so slightly, my English was improving. I started using the days that I had off to come in and ask if they needed any help just so I could learn a little more.

Obviously, there were some people who didn't understand why I wasted my time going in and working for free. Heck, sometimes I even questioned it myself. But I knew that what I was gaining was so much more than my overall loss. Through the extra time that I worked, I gained more experience throughout the kitchen besides sudsy wet dishes.

On one occasion, I remember that one of the main men who worked in the kitchen suddenly stopped showing up. Now when this happened, the main owner of the bakery was in a state of confusion because he was unsure what to do without his guy. Luckily, for me, I had a pretty good relationship with one of the employees, and he brought up the fact that I came there to work on my days off, and that I basically knew everything that the job would require me to do. I could see it in the owner's eyes—the doubt and contemplation. He wondered if I could really handle the task. I won't lie. I hardly expected to be accepted into the position, especially considering my main job had been cleaning dishes for the previous three months. To my surprise, he gave me the job, and after that, I kept continuously escalating up the totem pole until, at about eight months in, I was put in charge of basically the whole kitchen.

Of course, I was happy at this point that I was moving up in life, but being optimistic all the time is nearly impossible and having worries and emotions get to you is inevitable. I worried about the choices I had made and about where I was going to go. I would get home exhausted and would just lay and think about everything.

Thinking about staying in the same place forever, never really progressing by any means at all, having my parents' faces cross my memory and remembering the long days where I could just see the life being drained from them, and they wouldn't even flinch . . . these were not things I would accept.

I thought about how I never wanted to just conform to something because it was safe or available because I had too much ambition to have it just thrown away. But most of all, I remembered my mother's words before I left: to be good and always work hard. Having those consistently playing in my head allowed me to continue working and to keep faith that I was going to survive and make it.

Soon enough, after working many jobs, I finally had a coworker with whom I had a very strong love/hate relationship. In all honesty, I actually really liked the man, but he had a very strong personality that often-caused bumps in the road for me, but I always thought he was very intelligent and an overall great person. I might say that we were even friends who were close enough to be partners, and that is how I entered the restaurant world. It is a power duo that has lasted through the test of time. It's a great dynamic that we have going on, too. He loves Mexican food, and I just so happen to make it; our partnership couldn't have been better.

If you were to ask me years ago if I ever imagined myself in this position the possibility wouldn't have even surfaced, but the power of God and the hunger of a destitute heart—and the love of family—are things that should never be questioned. They remain. And they lead us to the lives we were meant to live.

PUMPKIN FLOWER CREAM

By Juan Luis González

Oil as needed
3 blocks of butter
1 cup white onion in small squares
2 pieces of Chile Poblano
2 cups of pumpkin flower (fresh or in can)
4 cups of sour cream
4 leaves of epazote
coarse salt to taste
white pepper to taste

Preparation

1. Stir-fry the onion with poblano chiles (already seeded and cut in pieces) for a few minutes until they are tender.

2. Add the pumpkin flower and leave it for two minutes.

3. Add the sour cream and epazote.

4. Continue to stir-fry for about 4 minutes over medium heat.

5. Add white pepper and salt to taste.

6. After the four minutes have elapsed, all the ingredients are put into a blender to make into cream.

Ready to be accompanied with enchiladas, chicken or as in this case, fish.

EVERARDO MEJÍA

Matador Sazonador

11
Courage

I love being able to tell people about my childhood—my parents and those I grew up with because the most exciting part for me is telling them how I grew up a superhero.

Now, I know it may sound odd, even unbelievable, but it's true. My mother was a superhero. Now, as some of you see these words and begin to wrinkle your brows and the lines on your forehead begin to appear as you flip back-and-forth among the pages just to make sure that you read this right, allow me to redefine the qualities of a superhero. Then you can be the judge of all of it.

As a young child, a superhero was an extraordinary person,

someone who you could only dream of becoming one day—a person who could handle more, do more, was more of everything than anybody else around you. A superhero was the fusion of kindness and ruggedness. He or she had the ability of outsmarting the limits of regular people and being able to lead by example. Their mantra is not knowing if they can defeat every obstacle, but having the immense courage and bravery to accept the risk and choosing even the slightest possibility of success over the more realistic possibility of defeat.

A superhero doesn't stop being a superhero because they forgot their cape at home. In fact, sometimes a superhero's greatest power is their superior control over everyday skills.

My mother created, loved, and raised, seven children, ran eighteen local businesses, and did it all while her partner in life struggled in another country to help provide for the seven gifts she had presented the universe.

She taught seven children about honesty and hard work and placed them in a living situation that, although wasn't ideal, instilled within them the craving for something better in life. My mother truly was, and is, something unlike anything I've ever seen. Her cape was laced with the tears that ached for a better life than the one she had. She was tainted with the heat of sun rays that burned against her skin, constantly etching into her cells why it all must be done. Her cape was vibrant and beautiful but often left at home next to the cross at her bedside table that gave her the strength to do it all over again.

My mother is undoubtedly a superhero that was never the plot inspiration for any comic or the selling title for a blockbuster action film, but she was the greatest thing to happen to six other kids and me. The only issue is . . . I never wanted to be like her.

I'm not sure if it was the arduous days of feeling my stomach collapse against itself when there was nothing to eat or the feeling of desperation when we would ask our neighbors to spare some food when we had none that changed my outlook on life. Even though my mother (and the countless other women who have surrounded my life) taught me the hard work a woman could do and fueled my admiration towards the gender, there was one piece of teaching that my mother and father echoed at home that just didn't sit well with me: not only was it expected for us to grow up to be good hard workers, it was always advised to be good, hard workers for somebody else, and that's the last thing I wanted.

Growing up and seeing my parents constantly working without rest, and knowing that they didn't have the liberties to be able to drop those duties to really enjoy life, was a fate I didn't want nor would I allow to take place. Out of every lesson and value that was taught to me, this was the one I couldn't accept.

I couldn't accept living my life working to make somebody else's future. I knew it wasn't going to be a straight shot job being on my own, and that I would need to start off working underneath somebody, but I also knew that it would be necessary in order to reach my ultimate goal. Soon I started working with my uncles where I grew talents in some unexpected fields like construction and electrical, although I mostly focused on the electrical jobs. As I was doing this, I was still thinking about how to further improve myself and my lifestyle, to which the obvious answer became school.

At my university in Mexico, I began to study biology and further expand the realm of possibility for me. More than anything, that's what university did for me. As a top student in my class, I had already received a great deal of accomplishment just with that title, but life had something else in mind for me. Suddenly, I was offered a unique scholarship, a gift most don't receive that opened doors to a stupendous opportunity. It was a nationally-based scholarship that contained the chance to study and work in the United States with all my expenses covered. The only thing left to do once the news broke out was to accept the offer . . . right? Because who in their right mind wasn't about to accept that offer? A shot to take a starving kid begging his neighbors for leftovers to a cross country taught biologist. And all of these are valid judgments. In fact, they're the exact same thoughts that were running through my head seconds before I turned down the offer, and the reason may seem like something straight out of a teenage drama. University not only presented me with magnificent opportunities academically, but it also presented me with one of my greatest gifts to date: my wife.

At that time, I was 27 with my girlfriend who was itching to get married, and the lovely folks distributing said scholarship, enlightened me with the fact that marriage would only lower my chances at receiving it. I'm not quite sure if I had mentioned that part to my girlfriend before or after, but I do remember her just saying, "Well, that's fine, let's go. We'll both go," to which I sheepishly responded, "Yes, honey, but that's the thing. They don't want both of us. They only want one . . . " It was a hard moment for me because how do you tell the girl you're in love with, who also shares the same career as you, that this sudden luck has fallen into your hands, and for the moment, it only wants you. On top of that, how are you supposed to throw away all the goodness they have brought into your life suddenly because of a generous, once-in-a-lifetime scholarship. I just couldn't. So, I didn't. Instead, she had the idea of moving to Chicago. It was a place we both could be together, and ultimately, our marriage could actually go through.

At the age of thirty, we decided to move to Chicago where she would continue her career as a biologist, and I went to go reinstate my degree in biology at the University of Illinois.

When I went in, a part of me, of course, was nervous because it was walking away from a part so known and comfortable for something completely new. It was like trading in your hand for a claw. While the change, in a way, is subtle— the functions are still quite the same—you're still you, but it inevitably impacts your lifestyle.

When I came to the university, they were astonished by the amount of credits I had. At the time, the required amount at the university was 86, and I believe that I had a little bit over 150. I did have to take some general education courses, but nothing huge like I had presumed I would encounter. I took some classes here and there, and while reading books and turning in worksheets were never an issue, communication was.

Initially, I wasn't worried about speaking, given the fact that I had taken various English courses at the university level already (and had some of the best professors straight out of England.) When it came to speaking, I really was okay with it, until when in doing so, I began to get funny looks and even mockery from my peers. I began to doubt myself a lot, questioning whether it was my pronunciation, even though I had been commended for it many times before. Maybe my sentence structure was off. It seemed that I always ended up butchering something when it came to speaking English. It wasn't until some time later that I realized there were different forms of English just as we Hispanics know that Spanish in Mexico is different than the one in Spain.

Now, it's not to make it seem as if the languages were two complete opposites, but there are some words and expressions that are taken differently or don't even exist in each dialect. When it came time to actually speaking, I realized people were having trouble understanding me because I was speaking English that was taught to me by British professors. So, I was speaking English with a British dialect. It did, in a sense, give me some source of relief to know that it wasn't as if I had wasted my time learning the language, but the fact that it was more of a miscommunication still inflicted a lot self-esteem issues.

Now, when I had to speak, there was no denying a sense of being self- conscious, whether the snicker in the far back left of the room was directed toward me or because someone told a joke, whether they were looking so intently in my direction because your speech was really that moving or because they couldn't understand me... It was a lot at the moment, and it taught me how much you can really count on others because there were a lot of times where those people who you called your friends were actually the ones going behind your back and making the most jokes. So, it turned a sour note on my social connections. That was the last thing I wanted to have bring me down. I know there are always obstacles, but my mentality is that it's how you overcome them that counts. I knew that that wasn't what was going to bring me down, that I hadn't spent almost three years not talking to my mother while living in the United States just for the enjoyment of some people who engaged in cheap, rude entertainment.

Day by day, I continued going to school and at the same time working to push my family along. I had reached a routine of eat, sleep, school, repeat. It was so intense that our family started questioning my wife on my actual whereabouts. In the beginning, my wife could easily get by excusing my absence due to work, but after a reoccurring pattern was obvious, they found it hard to believe that I could actually be working so much. It made them believe I was being snobby, as if I was too good for a sizzling seasoned smoky carne asada on a June afternoon (trust me, I am not... no one is), and the craziest thing was that if it wasn't that then clearly "working" was just a cover-up, and my wife really needed to find out why I would come home half alive calling out for my bed.

Simply put, it was a long phase in our lives where life was just rough, but I was trying to provide for my family and create the future I wanted, one I knew we deserved.

Eventually, I earned my degree in computer science that I had received while taking some side classes in school. I started looking for a better job in that field, something that I knew would be able to bring more to the table.

I was hired in a computer services company that was basically run and owned by Indian individuals. This, in itself, was not the problem at all because I always found them to be very intelligent people who were the best in what they did, which is exactly what I wanted to be.

Once I started, I won't lie, a part of me was scared because I noticed that the majority of them spoke broken English or couldn't even understand the language, and, of course, none of them spoke Spanish either, and I most definitely did not speak Urdu. I didn't want to let language be a barrier to my future, but besides that, I also had a moment of self-doubt where I questioned if I was capable of performing the jobs they were doing. I wasn't sure of the system they used or of the programs they were used to. In essence, I was a blind sheep walking into group of foxes knowing who they were and aimlessly hoping I would blend in.

While being introduced, I realized the systems they were using were actually quite outdated, and then something magical occurred. I noticed several men working at computers trying to use a program they seemed unable to master. I walked over and took a look, and it seemed like life was finally beginning to turn out just right. To my luck, it was the same program that I had been trained on while I was studying my practice. Quickly, I offered my assistance to which they obliged, but I wouldn't doubt it if there were hesitant minds in the moment. The real magic started once everyone saw me maneuvering the program with the ease of riding a bike. As time passed, my rank within the company escalated.

I was viewed as an asset.

I continued helping others with the program and was basically the head person who dealt with all questions and concerns in terms of program use.

I loved my time there. I gained a lot of respect from all my colleagues and began to learn and enjoy their culture more and more over, but all things must end so that new ones may flourish.

My initial idea was to move on and open my own computer service company and pursue my talent. Through many trials and errors, things just didn't come about. So, here I was, not really fully this or fully that. I had a degree in this, but I started questioning if that was even my intention anymore. It's difficult enough being conflicted in your own thoughts, trying to find the meaning behind your own self, but it's even harder when it's no longer just you because that's what happened, my life was no longer just me.

There was a part of me that I wasn't conscious of, but that came out in times like these. It was the me who worked days and nights to provide for my family. It was the me that took low blows from life and was determined to turn them into success. The one that never asked anything of anyone so that one day I could truly say I did this that even though I had excellent role models growing up at the end I did. It I accepted each risk life presented me with a mentality of " I don't know how, but it'll happen." It was this part of me that continued to thrive and question and search until it finally found what it was looking for, and from that search came about the business that has placed me where I am today.

My roots and the food from home have always been a prominent way of remembering who I am and the people I come from, and it dawned on me that the seasonings of food, and of life are what add that extra special touch. Now, this wasn't just me being nostalgic, but it was me realizing that I wanted to be able to create and distribute those seasonings. Without further deliberation I made my choice and began my journey, a journey that although seems to have started recently, has really been in the making all my life. It's been a long and hard one with many lessons that have molded me into who I am and have taught me of the important things in life. The most valuable thing to me is being able to now share it with everyone around me.

CORUNDAS

By Everardo Mejía

Corundas
1 kg of preferably yellow corn mass
250 grs of pork lard
½ cup warm water
1 tablespoon of salt
1 pinch of baking soda
1 cup ground rice
30 leaves of cane of corn

1. Mix all the ingredients in a uniform way until you get a consistent mixture.

2. Preheat a tamale pot with water.

3. The secret is to fold the cane leaves from a lower end and place the dough and fold triangularly then cook them.

This is accompanied with sour cream to taste and pork meat in tomato sauce.

HORTENSIA GUADARRAMA

La Quebrada Restaurant

—

12
Resilience

All I could think about was the bead of sweat slowly swelling at the ridge of my hairline, carefully dancing in a daring motion as if it were deciding whether it wanted to part ways with its origin or not. I started to feel the slight tickle of its downward route, and automatically my thought was to wipe away its existence, but I quickly remembered that I had no time. I had not a second to waste, and that bead of sweat could slowly turn into tears if my time is wasted. I threw away the thought of that ball of sweat along with the one streaking down my back and neck as I hurried to finish my grandfather's dinner. It hadn't been long since I started living with him—

my dream home not even in a million years—but I guess some sort of home is better than being an orphan, which is what I was.

After my mom died and my father left us, where else was a five-year-old supposed to live but with the closest of kin? In a way, I should be grateful that I had some family to call my own and that I was able to share a home with them, but my grandfather didn't grant me that security.

His form of life and discipline came from a very abusive and macho standpoint. His views were strong and harsh like the beatings he would inflict on his sons, like the ones that my skin can recall when, as a young girl, I failed to understand his right from wrong. Besides that, I was also appointed the woman of the house, performing every traditional domestic duty there was—from cleaning dishes, to cooking, to taking our clothes to the water, to cleaning everything.

There were nights when I questioned the universe's intentions and why it would predestine this for me. At too young an age, I questioned what I had done to deserve this. I would look through the window at the poor city in front of me, the dusty roads I took to school and the overcast sky that seemed to permanently dim the sun's light over my town. During moments like these, I envisioned my life far away from here, somewhere where I could finally be a child that these bitter circumstances had prohibited me from. This treatment kept going until finally when I was about eight or nine years old, my dad finally came to rescue me.

I think a part of him saw the actual situation I was in, and so he decided to bring me to live with him. It was a moment of shock and happiness for me. I just couldn't believe the twist of fate that my own father, who had initially left me, would come to save me and take me back. I tried not to question it too much because, in all honesty, I was not one to be choosy right then. As far as I was concerned, I could admire my grandpa's work ethic, but that's about it. I don't have many happy memories living with him, life with my father was a large step up than with my grandfather, but it was far from a real "home." Included with my dad's departure came a new wife—a new wife who didn't like my father's new-found child and was constantly working toward finding a way of getting rid of me.

At the age of thirteen or fourteen, she started pushing ideas of me finding possible suitors so that I could get married and finally leave. So, there I was, a young teen who had already been tormented by a rage-driven grandpa and now an evil stepmother who wouldn't rest until she saw her new husband's daughter out of the picture.

My only escape was the few days my aunt would take me to her home where I would help in any way she needed. They were my days of bliss, and, although they included hard work, I was in an environment where I could see a life much better than my own. When I would return to my father's house, I would start counting down the days until I would leave again. This cycle continued for some time until my aunt finally offered me the opportunity to come stay with her and help her out with her kids and other projects she had at hand. I didn't waste two seconds to capture my breath in order to say yes. Instead, I responded with a glistening smile of joy and hope because finally something was going right. I had been to my aunt's house countless times before. I was able to adjust quite quickly, but it was a completely new experience to wrap my head around that there was no going back this time.

This was my new life. Well, at least it was for some time. It was a life I loved until one day a lady mentioned to my father how her sister in Mexico City needed someone to help her around her home and with her new baby and was any way that he could send his daughter (me) to help out? My father agreed, which in a sense was a bit odd to me considering he wasn't one to keep me home, but he was more than open to send me off to work with whoever offered. I think my dad knew that I didn't want to be stuck in the same place day after day and that I wanted to leave. So, in his defense, he might have believed he was only doing what made me happy, but the possibility of just a happy functional home would have sufficed.

In any case, I started working with this family and although it wasn't much, it gave me a place to live and sleep and eat. If we're being honest, I wasn't as optimistic as I sound here. I was young and living like a peasant. I didn't get paid for doing the work I was asked to do. I guess people from where I come just look for something to do, a job to have, and are satisfied with whatever treatment comes with it.

In part, I was doing exactly what I had said would never be my path.

I learned to pretend that a cold ceramic floor was a warm, luscious mattress and that the wooden tabletop was a whimsical canopy. When it got cold, I curled up underneath my light bed sheet imagining it as a thick cotton wool bedspread, and this is what I was satisfied with.

I didn't think of all the things I didn't have or never had because it would just take too long, and during those lonely nights resting under the kitchen table, the whole goal was to get some sleep. Instead of being hopeless, I thought of the fact that I was still breathing, that I still had time, and that I still had enough drive and hope in me to envision something other than the moment I was in.

These thoughts alone were the only way I would welcome sleep to my tired body. Then, slowly, as my body drifted into a state of unconsciousness, I would inevitably feel his hands like curious children slowly but surely travel up my shirt searching, as if they were in desperate need for something to hold on to. Just like that, I was no longer searching for a way to be still, but a way to move. To move every part of him off me or a way to move every part of me out of his grasp. I wasn't trying to be picky, I just wanted to be safe. My boss's brother was a twenty-year-old looking to take advantage of a poor thirteen-year-old housekeeper who didn't have any other choice but to stay, and because my choices were so limited, I did.

That is, until I met a lady who mentioned to me about another family who had just moved from France. They were desperately looking for someone to take care of their home, and I was just plain desperate. I contemplated the situation. I wondered: Do I really want to jump into another strange family who I had no knowledge of? At least I knew what I was dealing with at the time. I figured the woman saw my doubt through my expression and quickly asked me, "Well, what are they paying you where you're working?"

My brows quickly curled in confusion at the sound of pay. I didn't know what she meant by that. Pay? I've never been paid for the work that I've done. My pay was having a home to call my own and food to eat, enough to keep me alive, but receiving money in exchange was a bewildering idea.

I, in a concerned voice responded, "No, I don't get paid anything . . ." At the sound of that, I believe she became even more astonished than I was. "What do you mean you don't get paid?! They have to pay you for what you do. You should be getting paid for putting in work! This is exactly another reason you should come with this family. I've heard they're nice people and they're willing to pay 600 pesos weekly."

Now that money, converted, may not be a ton, but you have to understand that I was coming from quite literally nothing to the most pay I had received in my lifetime. I deliberated for a little bit but ultimately decided to leave, mostly due to the fact that my boss's brother didn't understand the concept of boundaries and because I felt my body was beginning to lose the battle. At the age of fourteen, I began to work for this French family, who to me even now, has become a blessing to my life.

They were a family who lived through the war in France and ironically moved their family to Mexico in order to provide their children with a better future. Now, I say ironically because typically it's the United States where people go to find their better future, but that just goes to show that Mexico is no one's second best. I loved that family because I never once felt like their employee. In fact, I felt like one of the family. I remember the French mother asking me to rest with her in her big soft couches in the living room on late afternoons just so she could stay and chit chat with me about her life story growing up in France. The mother owned a very successful beauty salon where only very important people went to be pampered. The father wasn't the actual biological father but the man who took the lovely French woman's heart and ownership over her family.

He was the one I spent most of my time with since he maintained the home and cooked the most delicious meals. I felt as though I was an exclusive member of the family since he would show me how to prepare each dish and would share even the most top-secret family recipes with me. It was like I was holding a little piece of them and no one knew the precious gem snuck away in the corner of my pocket just for me. I cherished every moment I spent with that family learning, laughing, and receiving the support and encouragement to continue through life. I had never received any of this before.

At the age of seventeen, I finally decided to part from the family. It became such a heartache because it wasn't just quitting to find a new job, it was separating with the only family I had ever known. But with the time I had spent in the city of Mexico, I had entered the sphere of being young and in love and met a special man, one whom I would share an eternal bond with as the father to my children, a man who would intend to sell me the sun and the moon all in the name of love, but haggled his offer down to darkness and hell in the same way.

Love of his kind was not what I expected. I never imagined myself curled up in the corner of a room, arms crossed as if trying to emulate the Holy Spirit through my body while shielding myself from every blow. These are not the cinematic honeymoon scenes my mind was infatuated with or the perfectly paired lovey dovey monologues that erupted at the start. I recognized that. I truly did. I knew that this was no longer love and that I no longer wanted to be somebody's rag doll when they throw a tantrum and then act like it was all okay. I just didn't want to imagine that my resiliency to get this far was all for nothing.

As much as I tried to leave through multiple attempts, there was always a part of him who came out and begged for forgiveness, a part that swore everything had changed, that he recognized his wrongs and he wanted to get better, but he only wanted to be that with me. In those moments, in the midst of packing my bags, and being steps from the door, I would look back and question everything that possibly went wrong. I thought of every mistake I had ever made, I began to question whether it was my fault and if I was the one who was too headstrong to see her mistakes.

Was it possible that I was the real problem? It seemed that the longer I waited, the more doubts came to mind, and then, I would make the biggest mistake: I would look into his eyes.

I would see the man I fell in love with. I saw what at that moment seemed like regret, and I couldn't help but think that maybe this time it would be different because it didn't seem fair that through years and years of giving so much I would just walk away with nothing. Our story continued after all. He was the father of my children and together we decided to immigrate to the United States for a better future. I remember our voyage being . . . tight. I was squished. Underneath my feet were a couple and my husband at the time in the trunk of the truck of a man who offered to cross us over. As I was sitting next to the man, I could see that everybody seemed very nervous and, to be quite honest, being so young I didn't quite understand everybody's worry.

I had left my son with some people by the border due to complications of having to cross at the time. It was an agreement that they would bring him to me once I was across because they had more experience with such things, and it was much easier getting kids across with fake documents. Given this clarity, I felt much better about my choice to move, but once I arrived, days and days passed by and the same question kept popping up about why I couldn't get my son back. They kept telling me to wait, that they were waiting for the right time, but it seemed to me that the right time never came. I begged and pleaded for them to return my baby, who at the time was only one-year old, but they just refused. It wasn't until one day when I finally had enough that I blew up, and their paranoia, combined with the scene I'd made, finally convinced them to return my child after about four days.

I figured my major struggles had finally begun to diminish, but it was my naiveté to not notice that they were only just beginning. While I had plenty of classmates and friends who constantly spoke of family members who traveled to the United States and worked all these hours and got paid all this money, much more than what was accustomed from where I came from, the script they gave me was straight out of Hollywood. It did not exist.

Coming to this country was set up to be a dream, and I had fallen for that dream. I thought of all the hours I was going to work, of the late nights I would spend accumulating checks to provide for my family, and I dreamt of the happy ending when we would finally have enough to return home and live a better life than the one we left behind. Everything that I expected to happen fell through the cracks, and everything that I never expected replaced it.

Years later, I finally left my husband and through time, I met a man who I married in a green card marriage. This man is the one who initially supported me with my restaurant- La Quebrada- together, we opened our first location and though everything did not come out as expected, it was quite all right. The thing is, there are some people who don't know how to handle power, who feel as if they have the control and right of power over anyone, and they end up spreading disaster like a disease. The man who, at the time, was my husband became corrupt spending all of our money, owing our rent, leaving me without any employees— basically sending my restaurant's name to the ground and leaving me with nothing. And to top it all off, he placed me in charge of everything and suddenly vanished.

At this point, I had no time to cry about my misfortune. Instead, I fully invested myself in my kitchen. I worked every day with a family member to bring my location up from its shambles. Every day I was cooking new recipes, asking people to try them and to tell me which they preferred. It was a slow process, but it's a process that has brought me to where I am now and because of that, I would repeat it all.

I'm not just an orphan girl who has been forgotten, I am a woman whose passion fuels a life of love, and for that I am thankful.

LA QUEBRADA STYLE CHICKEN BREAST
By Hortensia Guadarrama

La Quebrada Style Chicken Breast
2 large chicken breasts
2 tomatoes (cooked)
1 jalapeño pepper (roasted)
1 clove of garlic and 6 ounces of cheese
Salt to taste

1. Season your chicken breasts.

2. Cook them in a hot pan with a little oil,turning them until they are cooked.

3. At the same time, cook chiles and tomatoes.

4. After they're cooked, liquefy, and add salt.

5. Put your breasts in a baking dish add the ingredients liquefied tomato, chile and garlic, add on top 3 ounces of Chihuahua cheese, on each chicken breast cover when the cheese is gratin.

ALICIA ROMERO HERNÁNDEZ

Café de Alicia

13
Humility

My mother, with her three businesses, was always very busy. Day after day she was always doing business of some kind, selling this and that and for special events or holidays, her income would sometimes triple. Well, this was one of those days. The kermes (flea market) had come to town, a day where we pay tribute to our saints and sell even more than usual, so we can have an offering for them. It all becomes sort of a big event in town, whether it be extra vendor stands or games, and even music.

The point is, the kermes was here, I was here, we were in the same place together, and I most definitely was ready for it. Every time it came around, my other eight siblings and I loved going, especially the younger ones. This time was no different. All we could think about during the day was when we were going to head down there. I could already imagine the paved and rocky roads lined with vendors from all over. I started sorting through the toys and cool products they would bring and set up my own mental shopping spree.

I could smell the street food filling every crevice to ensure that we always knew it was present, and I got excited at the thought of seeing all my other friends playing around in the streets with the lovely music as a backdrop. Once we were all done with chores and helping my mom, we started to get ready to go. At this point, everybody was busy just doing their own thing. Suddenly, I had a very impulsive idea, one I find very hard to forget. I figured with eight kids, money for that day might not have been available, so I gave myself the task of finding it for myself. The only mistake I made was finding it in my mom's room . . . in the box where she kept her earnings for the day . . . and taking it without permission. In my mind, it seemed like a foolproof plan—after all, she had made a lot of money that day. I didn't see how she would notice a few bills missing or much less figure out which of us nine had done it.

So, I carried along this thinking at that time. I thought I was very slick for the work I had done until my mother rounded all of us by the front door. A harmonious chorus of hurried stomps and gleeful giggles slowly consumed the room that abruptly subsided once they met my mother's face.

"Alright, kids, I want all of you right here. I'm going to give you each some money so you can have fun."

My stomach dropped, and my heartbeat shot up to about 300

beats per minute. Basically, I went numb and cold, and suddenly the few bills crumbled in my back pocket transformed into thirty-pound cement blocks. I tried my best to maintain a straight face while a full-fledged meltdown was being played out in my head. I started thinking of all my possible escape routes. Well, there's that door behind me, but I have too many people behind me. Or, there's always the front door, but that's too far, and she already has the advantage. Or, if worse comes to worse comes to worse, there's always the side window . . .

I also started to weigh my options on explanations, whether I should just come clean or construct some elaborate explanation on how her money coincidently went from her box to my back pocket.

Being so consumed with my worrying, I had zoned out of the situation until I heard my mom question all the little faces staring back at her on who had taken her money?! In a panic, I began to slyly step away from the group toward a family member that was there accompanying us. My mindset at this point was "What she doesn't know won't hurt her" . . . or so I thought.

I, with my sweet charm and the innocence of a youngster, convinced her that my mom had previously given me the money and that I needed her to take care of it for me. All was going well until the family member passed by mom just before we left and mentioned that I had given her money given to me to watch over, money from my mother. Now, I know she was just being polite and letting my mother know, but, Jesus, it had been going so well.

So, my mother promptly smiled at her and looked back at me with a look that screamed anything but fun. I already knew in my head that whatever plans I had for the night had just vanished, but you can't help but have that fleeting sense of hope, right? That night, I kneeled in front of the little wall where we have all of our saints adorned, for the duration of the time it took for my siblings to come back home. Considering they left around 6 p.m. and didn't come home until about 10 p.m., that's about four hours of picture perfect church posture right there.

My mother warned me not to move a muscle and to pray to the saints for forgiveness for my act of theft.

Out of all the things I could've done, this was by far the worst—not because it was so extreme, which I know some of you may be thinking—but because my mother always taught us to never steal. She taught us that you cannot take what somebody else has worked for and call it yours. It was something that she always voiced to us. So, stealing from her box of money was most likely going to be given as an offering to the church. Obviously, I clearly did not think my plan through.

Although that is a lesson and moment in time that I will never forget, it doesn't overshadow the countless amount of times I spent kneeling and vulnerable, mourning my father's death. At the age of six, I became the child of a single mother whose story was never meant to pan out that way.

I held on to vague memories with my father. Like the typical life on a ranch munching on delicious fruits like watermelon and cantaloupe when the season came along and the heart of his laugh expanding from his chest into every crevice of our kitchen as we ate my mother's delicious guisados. It was not only a time of a pain but a testing trial to see just how far each one of us could stand through life.

There was an immense vacancy that took over my insides that was impossible to ignore. I was the youngest of nine children not only battling the loss of my father but of any possibility of having that "daddy's little girl" relationship. I was robbed of strong arms and an eternal protector being forced to be okay with whatever the universe deemed right for me. The transition of life continued to sting but slowly began to lose its strength as an uncle of mine took over that role. Now, I shouldn't say "took over" because I will forever only have one dad, but my uncle did as much as he could to not completely vanish the vacant spot in me; at least it soothed the loneliness.

Through time, you adjust to the life you are given, but no one will ever compare in strength to my mother because as we all mourned, she cut our grievance in half and continued to push day in and day out to reinstate every last morsel of normalcy our lives still had. She was the woman who worked nonstop and did it with a smile, never giving you the slightest doubt of the authenticity of her happiness. It was through her that I learned the true meaning of hard work and courage. It was through people like my mother and grandparents that my happiest moments stem from. Whether it be the day of my quinceañera, where every care was thrown out the window feeling as the beautiful threads of my princess style gown dressed not only my being but the vision of my mother's eyes racing through my head, to the day my sons packed their final bag before our big departure into our next unknown.

At the age of twenty, my mom's last words of care consisted of a lot of, "I love you's" and "Please take care of yourself." With a long slow breath, I smiled and promised her I would. To this day I've accomplished her last task for me, but it's not as if there weren't times when the memory of her radiated through my smile. Or the days spent in my grandparents' restaurants working hand in hand as a family, all striving together as one to keep our bond. It's all of these moments stirred together that remain in me.

When I crossed over the border, I had a seven-year-old son at the time, but due to regulations, he was simply put on a plane and brought over to stay with family until I arrived. So his journey started and ended much faster than mine. Even though I didn't feel as if my journey was as bad as others, it's still an event in time that has marked my life for an eternity. It's not easy to forget four days of walking across the desert, accompanied by days of swimming as well. It's not easy to forget the feeling of ache as your now nail-less toes begin to throb because of the days of no rest and nights of almost peaceful sleep. Or, the drying bodies of people, just like me, who did not reach their final destination—unless it was decomposition under the sun dissolving into the desert's hand. So, when the air would blow and grains of sand would fly, I felt their hearts beating against my skin. A quick anxious beat followed by a sudden calming fall that soon turned into nothing. It was a quick subtle touch, but I swear I felt it. It's even harder to forget the emotion of joy once I arrived, a part of me debating whether this was real life because in this reality, I had made it. In this reality, my life was starting. And whether it was true or not, this was the reality I was choosing to stay in.

It only took three days for me to find work in my new home, and honestly, I could say it was my mother's working hands and push in making us experience the real world that landed me that opportunity. I started off in a bakery owned by an American couple, my experience only stemming from my passion of cooking and endless hours in our family restaurant. But other factors, such as basic knowledge of the language, the only true form of communication, were nonexistent. It was

CHAPTER 13 - ALICIA ROMERO HERNÁNDEZ

a phase of constant repetition. I was in charge of fetching ingredients for the woman while she prepared whatever pastry was set to be made, easy enough, right? Well, it would be if I knew what to fetch or understood what it was she was asking me to do. It seemed like a nice little game going on. She would ask me for milk and I would bring her eggs. She would ask me for eggs and I would bring her milk. She would always ask me for eggs and I seemed to always bring her milk until one day it seemed as if all the days of frustration and oblivion began to slowly dissipate. The days of coming home and writing in my little journal phrases and translations began to pay off, and that in itself, gave me the confidence boost I needed to continue to push for, not only my future, but my sons' futures as well.

My bond with my bosses gradually grew after that as well as my role in the bakery. There were occasions where my bosses would leave me in charge of making the pastries while they were out on vacation and something about the trust that cultivated between us gave me hope that my future could be elevated so much further than I had originally imagined. It was as if that drive to be better emanated through my work, something that I assume caused a restaurant chef who visited the bakery to steal me from my job post there. It was a chef who complimented my work ethic and promised me so much more than what my present-day job offered. It was an offer that I couldn't resist. And in the time span of four months, I was working alongside the pastry chef of an Italian restaurant making up to $1,000 a week, a wage that made my bakery job seem like an allowance.

In an unfortunate twist of fate, the arm of the pastry chef was severely burned, a burn that wiped the majority of the meat from his bones and left him incapable of working. It was within this time that my boss called me into his office causing me to question everything that I had done wrong that would cause him to demand my presence in his office. It was a worry that quickly faded once he offered me the new position of top pastry chef, and a feeling of elation that almost as quickly replaced it. A feeling of elation that didn't last as long as I hoped due to the divorce of the owners and the downfall of the restaurant that soon followed.

It seemed as if I was finally getting to the top and, at a moment's notice, I was back to ground zero. The only jobs that were available during those times were paying a measly $7.50 an hour. Coming from a job that was paying me up to $30 an hour at times, my life could not function under the lower pay wage. Under the sudden conflict and frustration that my life had now come under, I decided to open my own business on the local streets of my town and take destiny into my own hands. During my time as a street vendor selling tamales, I decided I not only wanted to advance financially, but I wanted to expand my knowledge. So, I enrolled in college first, tackling the language, obtaining the equivalent of a high school education, and finally ending with culinary education.

After my time as a vendor, I finally established a set location to always be instead of moving from place to place. I loved it. I loved having our own little nook where customers came and knew who we were and continued to come because they genuinely enjoyed what I was serving. After about two years of having my tamales in a set building, I got an amazing opportunity from a Jewish family who owned a flea market who had never had a food concession within their business. They told me of how they spent days looking through the internet trying to find a vendor and stumbled upon all the great reviews our lovely customers had left. Ultimately, they offered me a spot within the market, and I went from full time tamaleria to a week job there and a weekend job at the market. It was an amazing opportunity that I am forever grateful to have received, but after two to three years of paying rent and working at the flea market, I decided to finally find our own building to call ours and only ours. We went from being the top half of a building standing over a banquet hall to having our own full-fledged restaurant on the main floor and our humble home on top.

The feeling of owning something and having the capability of saying that it's truly and entirely yours is unlike any other. After each hardship that I had passed—the constant separation of family, the trips I took walking and swimming time and time again just to visit my mother when she lived...then died. It should not have surprised me that after her death, every person in town decided to come eat. And to this day, I have yet to see my restaurant as full as that day. It's the fact that this restaurant is so much more than just hard work; it's my life and love for family painted onto the walls and my mother's arms wrapped around the structure breathing life into each dish that she inspired. My passion for what I do that brings it all together.

It's how every day the restaurant is not just a restaurant but a place where my kids grew up playing with the other little kids in town. It is filled with the love of family I grew up with. It's knowing that I've worked hard not only for myself, but in order to leave something for my children. It's everything that blossomed from a little table on the side of the street that has made our kitchen and Alicia's kitchen Cocina de Alicia.

CHILE DE CIRUELA

By Alicia Romero Hernández

Chile de Ciruela (Plum)

2 lb. pork meat
3 garlic cloves
1 large slice of onion
3 leaves of Laurel.
½ teaspoon thyme
½ teaspoon marjoram
sauce
8 tomatillos
4 chilies jalapeños
1 lb. of plum
1 slice thick onion
2 cloves garlic
1 pinch of pepper
1 tablespoon of salt

1. In a saucepan put the meat to cook with garlic, the big slice of onion, bay leaf, thyme, marjoram salt, and water until the meat is covered.

2. Once its cooked separate it from the broth and only the meat is left to the fire to be cooked in its own fat.

3. The broth is reserved.

4. With very little water, cook the jalapeño with the tomatillos until they are cooked well. And later blended with the pepper, onion, garlic and cumin.

5. In a separate pot, put some water with the plums until they are cooked.

6. At the end of this process, drain the water and mash the plums a little.
7. In the pan where the meat is fried, put the sauce and plum and meat broth and let boil for 15 min.
It is ready to be served.

PABLO PINEDA

El Patio Latin Restaurant

———

14
Love of Culture

It's a chilly Chicago winter afternoon, and lunch rush has just passed. The only remnants of the existence of people is the stack of dirty plates that have been left as souvenirs on their tables as if to say, "Hello, don't forget me. I was here and real." The staff and I run over to answer their calls while emptying whatever leftovers were smeared across the plates.

The sudden clatter of metal forks scraping against colorful plastic plates reminds me of a familiar tune that is only brought together by the hearty laughter of coworkers discussing the day's work. The separate sounds unite as one with the sizzling of a pan in the background singing from the kitchen. It's a sound too familiar to me, a sound I can't quite put my finger on . . .

It reminds me . . . it reminds me of home.

I see images of miles and miles of greenery draping over the land stealing the show from the blanket of pebbles and stone that covered the ground. And beyond that, I feel the ominous power of a gigantic mountain standing tall behind me.

I begin to meditate and recall things that haven't crossed my mind in too long.

My dirt home in Guatemala comes to mind with a stream of about fourteen dogs barking and running around, their sights and sounds becoming a signature for us. My father would either be at work in the back of the house repairing something, and my mother would probably be at his side helping him with his carpenter job. In the meantime, I would circle the many fruit trees we had, aimlessly trying to choose between peaches, guavas, cherries, and God knows what else we had hiding for a lunchtime snack. If it wasn't doing that, I would be somewhere off in the middle of streets going against my friends in a hardcore soccer tournament with a makeshift branch goal.

I grew up in an area where you invented your entertainment, and there was always something to do. Now, that statement held truth not just because we had plenty of land to work with but because we had parents who always gave us something to do. Of course, there were simple things like taking care of the home, but other times it was my father attempting to teach us things about carpentry that pretty much went in one ear and out the other thanks to the rebellion of a young mind that didn't really find an interest in nails and wood.

The biggest blessing was my grandmother.

My grandmother was a wonderful human being. She was not able to walk any more due to complications within her veins and lungs. She was the closest thing to a saint on earth and the most committed Catholic I have yet to meet. Because of her outstanding commitment and stubbornness, she refused to let something so trivial as not being able to walk (I say it with as much nonchalance as she lived it) stand in the way of her and her weekly service. Because she was stuck in a wheelchair and not able to go on her own, my parents automatically placed the responsibility on my brothers and me.

The saddest part was that no one wanted to do help her. We were in a place where you basically knew everyone, and to us it was embarrassing to having to roll her down to service because she couldn't walk. I mean literally you would have to pay someone for them to even consider it, and since I typically got stuck with the unwanted jobs, I was the lucky one.

At first, I begrudgingly obliged, silently taking her. My grandmother tried to make small talk, but my attitude got in the way of giving her anything more than a few word responses. Time passed and week by week, I started to get to know—really know—my grandmother. She was the most pacifist woman I've ever met. She refused to engage in any type of argument, much less a physical altercation.

She was just filled with such kindness and wisdom, and some of the things she said have become the pillars that hold me up to be the person I am today.

She never raised her voice or insulted others. Of course, there were moments she got irritated and upset, but through it all, she never was one to snap. She would tell us that God had given us the gift of speech, and if that was the case, we should welcome everybody and know how to use our gift well.

That's another thing she would always remind me of—to never question the things of God. I would sometimes look at her and begin to feel sorry for her inability to move her legs, and I would ask if she felt anger or sadness over it. She would look at me and say, "No, why? Everything is done in God's will. Nothing here is our own, not even our own bodies. My legs were a gift from God, and He knows and gets to decide how long I get them for. Everything is for a reason, and God knows why he does things."

I sometimes just stood back flabbergasted at what she said because I couldn't wrap my mind around the positivity of someone who has lost so much.

She was the woman who taught me about kindness and respect, a characteristic that, after the militias and internal wars started consuming Guatemala, seemed to be lost. It's a tragedy when the most beautiful places are quickly turned into the most horrific—all because of the arrogance and pride of man.

As a kid in school, we would get new kids all the time, children who were rescued from war centers who had lost everything except a second chance at life. The majority of them were indigenous people of Guatemala, people who were in the land of their people, but who were always treated as second-class citizens.

Whoever says that's it's not true, clearly is able to walk past the street posts full of indigenous people selling items, trying to make a living and still withstanding plenty of mockery to their faces. They must be able to ignore the snickers from a group of teens making snobbish indigenous jokes or the subtle change in formality when someone approaches their stands and refers to them in the informal "you" as if to automatically let them know that they are less to you because of some materialistic superiority you have granted yourself.

I hated that in class a boys pain and loss, a boy who had been saved by nuns while watching both the execution of his parents and sisters, was mocked. I hated that his tragedy wasn't enough for them, that on top of this forced misfortune, it was necessary for them to add their own pinch of salt to the wound.

So, after a few years, I created an organization where we help indigenous people learn basic principles that aren't available to them. Things like writing and speaking and basic schooling. At the same time, I was going to school and soon I graduated with a career in broadcasting in Guatemala. I was a reporter for a local show that gave anyone the opportunity of doing what I do. For example, we would take a random woman who was a baker and let her gather other people who were in the same profession, basically interview them, and go about sharing an event, etc. In that time in my life, things were pretty alright. I felt like I was doing my family proud. I was doing things that I loved, and, most importantly, I was in the country I loved.

I seemed to have landed in a state of happiness until the crime and violence in Guatemala became just too much. Typically, the people who were targeted were the upper middle class and rich families, those who seemed to obviously have enough fortune to bathe in. So what was wrong with vandalizing/stealing/holding a beloved family member for ransom and forcing a few thousands out of them?!

You would hear all kinds of stories of local shops being broken into and brothers, sisters, or even fathers being killed because a family refused to pay. Even the ones who did pay still were not guaranteed that their loved one would return home alive . . . or whole. While the chaos was horrific, and my family lamented for them, we never truly thought we could be a potential victim.

We didn't have anything to offer them. No fancy house or car or million-dollar savings bank. We were just a humble family in a rural area with nothing to give. So, when we saw that the vandals had become so desperate that they were kidnapping just about anyone they thought they could get even the slightest amount of money out of, I unfortunately, knew it was my time to leave.

I headed to the United States like a lot of other Latinos under the assumption of a quick stay—enough to buy myself a car and make some money to support my family. I of course, like many other immigrants, was incorrect.

I thought of my organization in Guatemala and saw that nothing like that was being done here. I knew it was something I wanted to incorporate, so I began the construction of it. Some way, somehow, I didn't want to leave Guatemala behind in Guatemala. I carried it everywhere with me, in my thoughts, my heart, and in my blood. I found that the most potent way of keeping all that alive with me was through the food that I had enjoyed in my lifetime. That's how I came up with the idea of building my restaurant. And I've said it many times, that even though I'm not the best cook, I have the heart to put enough love and devotion into my plates.

I had wonderful people here who made my dream possible, and after some time I was able to get my parents to transfer their lives to the U.S. and leave our beautiful home, gated with aromatic trees, behind.

To this day, my mother is the one who teaches the cooks how to make the plates the most authentic they can be.

THE GUATEMALAN MOLE

By Pablo Pineda

The Guatemalan Mole is a delicious dessert made with ripe banana which has its origin from the middle of the sixteenth century. It is a perfect example of the fusion between Indians and Spaniards, since the chocolate is of Mayan origin and the other ingredients are of Spanish origin.

6 bananas
2 seeds of pepitoria
20 ripe tomatoes
5 chiles pasilla
2 cinnamon sticks
2 champurradas
8 ounces of chocolate
2 ounces sesame

1. Put the bananas to fry.

2. Simmer tomato, chile and cinnamon, stir and mix while cooking. Then let cool.

3. Meanwhile brown the pepitoria and sesame.

4. Put in a blender the tomatoes, chiles, cinnamon, pepitoria, sesame and champurradas (Guatemalan sweet bread)

5. Put this mixture in a bowl and add the chocolate. Stir until it is well mixed.

6. Add the fried bananas to absorb the flavor of the mixture and the chocolate.

7. Let it cool and serve it decorated with sesame seeds and enjoy this delicious guautemalteco dessert.

(I add a little ginger to my reciper to give it a very special touch.)

EZEQUIEL FUENTES

Mi Tierra Restaurant

15
Work Ethic

My land is one of lush greens and cobblestone streets taking vanity to the next level. It is easily recognizable by its beautiful churches and towering palm trees that sway like the pedal of a metronome, as if mimicking the heartbeat of the city. My land greeted my grandparents' faces every morning for work and sang them lullabies just before bed so that they would never forget it. Its skies have seen my steps turn into leaps and has witnessed my falls from early on, but my land doesn't see me as much anymore..

We have a more distant relationship now.

It can no longer send me songs through the chirping crickets or send its love through either of my grandmothers' Mexican food—oozing smells that only served to tempt my stomach. I may not be so close to my land. I may not be able to reminisce in its liveliness or watch the sun come up from the horizon, but I will never be that far from my land because a few thousand miles is not enough to separate me when my heart is always in Mi Tierra.

There is one thing I know and hold to be true: if you think small, you can only really ever be small, but if you think big— which you always should—there's no telling the big things that lie ahead of you.

That is one lesson I will never forget from grandmother—that no dream or wish is too big, that your dream should always be bigger than the one before. I assume it stemmed from a place of wanting her grandchildren to go farther than her or even her children.

The composition of my family consisted of my parents and my grandparents from both sides. Both of my grandmothers were hardworking, tenacious individuals who didn't allow life to dictate what was going to happen but rather took life by the horns and steered it into the direction they saw fit.

Both were amazing cooks who owned their own Mexican stores where they had food and other goods.

My grandfather on my mother's side died and left my grandma alone as a widow. Though his death caused pain within the family, my grandma never let that deter her from working or continuing her life.

We often asked her why she continued to work, and we were often flabbergasted by her lack of fatigue after long days. One thing that did impact me the most was seeing my grandmother work every day, seven days a week. I never once saw her complain.

She never once said she was too tired or frowned upon any supplementary jobs, and when asked if she ever wanted to just rest because she must be tired, she, simply being the way she was, issued a response that wasn't anything less than fantastic. She said, "Tired for what?! Being tired isn't going to help me survive. It's not going to provide me with money. No one is going to give you money to be tired. People give you money to work and get the job done—a job well done."

And with that, my grandmother summed herself up in a nutshell. She continued her business as well as my other grandmother who wasn't a widow but had the same hard work ethic.

Both my grandparents on my father's side were very hardworking, but my grandmother did slightly outrank my grandpa in that aspect. When my grandfather lost his ranch, where he primarily made his living, instead of crumbling, my family figured it was up to us to figure out how we were going to help push things along. So, my father decided to migrate to the United States in search of a better paying job than what he had in Mexico.

Now, as an adult, I realize the sacrifice each and everyone has made for their families. Starting with my grandmothers who, at an early age, led by example as the images of diligence and obedience. They constantly showcased a go-to attitude of hard work and being the best person one could be.

My grandmother's most famous saying was, "If you gather with poop, its smell will start to stick with you." That was a nicer version of it, but overall it reminded me to steer clear of those who are going to inhibit me from actualizing those big dreams that I had.

And then there was my father who left his country and ventured off into less than desirable conditions in order to bring food to a table where he was not even present. After days and months of his absence, constantly looking at photographs and being told stories of him—as if I was trying to scrape up every piece of memory, every proof of existence that he was here—to maintain him in my mind in order to never forget him.

My mother was then playing the part of a single mother, and I can only imagine how difficult it must've been to not only take care of me but now be limited to a love that was only seasonal. You see, it was never a sure thing when and if my father was returning home, and when he did, it never seemed to be a long enough stay, and so finally at the age of eleven, my father decided to bring me with him.

A part of me was excited that I would finally be spending more time with my dad and getting to see and experience what my dad was spending so much time on. Besides that, it was my first time to the Untied States and out of my home. So naturally, bits of fear transcended into that same feeling of excitement. What started off as what I perceived as an out-of-country school trip, soon turned into the rest of my life. I initially thought that my trip to the United States was for school. I figured I would stay here a couple of years, learn new things, make new friends, learn a new language, adapt to a new way of life, and then naturally make my way back to the country I called home. But this is not the case at all. When I got here, I immediately joined the workforce which is funny because at the age of 11, I didn't even know that there was a workforce, much less that I would be in it.

How do you do that?! Are there uniforms? Do we get swords, passwords? … What the heck is the workforce?

I quickly learned that no, sadly there were no swords, but it came with all the hard work that I presumed my favorite action movie would've encompassed.

There were days where my father and I would return exhausted, just dreaming of a hot bath and clean sheets on our drive back home. I quickly learned the work of making a dollar and that my father wasn't here vacationing—that it wasn't as glorious as a people make it sound when they're in Mexico. That's the thing. When you're over there, you're constantly being fed stories of overnight millionaires, of how family members have migrated to this country that can easily be mistaken for Candyland because of how outlandish it's painted to be. How people come here and get to pick and choose their jobs—that they begin earning a six-figure salary within months—that it's full of opportunities unlike any other and that they can make a payment on a $1 billion home in the hills. That's just not the case, and I got to witness that first hand.

Sometimes you realize that it's not where you are that grants opportunities, but sometimes it's who you are that either opens access or denies it. This has to do with much more than just being Latino. Being an immigrant, being in a land that technically isn't your own it—it goes far beyond that because of course there are limitations and struggles that our people must overcome that aren't necessarily required for others. And yes, it's unfair, but that's just life.

One thing though, that you can control is how you decide to fulfill your life, and the type of mindset and mentality you want to emanate to the world.

I'm grateful for having beautiful and inspiring people around me who have filled me with such knowledge and strong inner values that have led me to the point where I am now. For example, my grandmother would always tell me, "Never think of yourself as better than anybody, but also never think of yourself as less than anybody. We all have a purpose here, we all matter equally, and you have every much a right to be where you want to be as the next person."

This has constantly been the fuel that has carried me along the roads I've travelled. Not only after working for some time here in the states and then eventually going into the business field—but just in general, even through my toughest times because life has a funny way of showcasing who's in charge.

Sometimes when you think you've found your forever person, life makes it it's mission to remind you that you don't get to choose when and what that means. The thing is, she wasn't just my wife, she was the woman for me. We were a team, and a pretty damn good one too, but our forever didn't last, and she left much too early.

The death of my first wife was quite a humbling experience that shed even more rays of truth to the saying that my grandmother has inscribed in my brain because it points out how you can have all the riches of the world, but your circumstances can easily end up being the same as the person right next to you even if you may believe that there's something that you have that they don't or vice versa.

It was only through dedication, hard work, practice and my faith that I have been able to overcome all of the obstacles that life has confronted me with. Of course, there are moments where I have to question how much farther I can go, but instead of questioning it, I simply ask the Lord to take me as far as He's willing because we need to trust that he will take us to where we need to go.

Thankfully, he has led me to this position which was buying my current establishment, " Mi Tierra" an iconic trademark of little village and to hundreds of latinos in the Chicago area. It has been a journey for sure, an adventure to be exact, but I wouldn't want it any other way. I always say that I love what I do, which is true. Well, more importantly I love food. I love eating, and I'm so lucky to be constantly surrounded by all of those things and call it my job.

With my restaurant ,I have been able to capture our Mexican culture and transcend it into the modern atmosphere of today while still maintaining old traditional values.

I want to leave something for not only my children to remember, but future generations to come. I want to welcome you to my land, Mi Tierra.

MOLE DE GALLINA

By Ezequiel Fuentes

Mole de Gallina
8 ozs de puya
Half pound of guajillo chile
Half pound of sesame
8 oz of pumpkin seed
2 tablets of chocolate
8 oz of raisins
3 bananas
2 oz of cinnamon
3 green tomatoes
3 red tomatoes
6 cloves garlic
2 small onions
1 tost roll
8 oz of peanuts
Pinch of cumin
2 whole chickens
Chicken broth

1. Fry the Chiles, fry the ingredients and mix in the blender with the spices and chicken broth.

2. The chicken is cooked with a little water until it is covered and add salt, onion, garlic.

3. The ingredients that we blend in the blender put them to fry in a large saucepan with a large spoonful of butter. Constantly stir so it does not stick and when it starts to boil, let it boil for 3 min.,

4. Then integrate your chicken pieces let it cook for a few minutes, and it's ready to serve.

DANIEL GUTIÉRREZ
Cantón Regio and Nuevo León

16
Gratitude

To my sons. What if I told you Christmas doesn't exist?

Better yet, what if I just failed to mention its existence so your mind wouldn't even ponder its arrival?

What if I told you that, on that odd day when all of your friends suddenly appear with new toys and fresh clothes, this universal holiday is all part of your imagination? That there was no plump man with a snowy beard and beet red cheeks prancing in a blood red velvet suit distributing gifts and that he just so happened to miss your house.

What if . . . what if I/we/you just couldn't bear the thought of watching your young eyes droop down and the corner of your cheesy grin slump and one could see the fight between your instinct that was taking place as you forcibly swallowed your own tears? What if I just didn't want to break your heart again? What if I couldn't bear to add something else onto the list of all the things you could not have, yet deserved so much?

So, no, I will not tell you there is Christmas. I do not know who Santa Claus is, and gifts are out of the question.

. . . but maybe, just maybe, next year will be a different story.

I knew from an early age that family was like a well-oiled machine. In order for us to grow and succeed as a unit, each individual had to put their share in, and this wasn't a choice, it was a necessity.

I learned the art of sacrifice because it was always exhibited throughout my household, painted on my disheveled walls, and engulfing my mother's spirit. I watched as she made jobs out of life: making tortillas, washing clothes, or ironing for strangers—all to move us along day by day. Quickly, we learned that the only day that we were really going to get anywhere was by joining her. So my three brothers and I cooperated in any form that we saw fit.

I personally went out to sell gum around the streets and to my little friends, or on some days, I offered shoe shining to grown men with all of the lavish luxuries I couldn't even dream of having. Nothing was off the table—anything that needed to be done to help my parents was done, and it was a helpless act because there was never anything we asked for in return. Work was just a deed as necessary as breathing and we knew that.

At the time, we had a father who crossed the border and was

working in Texas. He was striving to give us something that was too out of reach in our homeland. I won't say I was raised by a single mother because my father was always present in some way. (It wasn't as if we were abandoned.) But there was enough reality present for us to understand that Dad wasn't going to be here every week to see us. In other words, we did become men very quickly, and my mom sure didn't get a fairytale relationship, but she never complained. She just adjusted to taking care of four boys while still maintaining her authority. That's one thing my parents never lacked—the power of showcasing who they were.

No one could even think of disrespecting my mother or her word because she had already established that she was not one to be played with. If you were to sass her, you would be punished. If you lied about where you were, you would be punished, and although my mother was the overall head of the house, because my father was always working, he still had a look that could make "Medusa" turn to stone.

Heavy as a stone is exactly how my heart felt when my mother told us to pack our bags because home would no longer be home.

A million thoughts raced through my mind as I started questioning everything, reminiscing through every detail I once thought tiny in importance, and now realizing they were everything. I worried, looking down at my leftover "machacado con huevo," wondering if that was the last time I would ever see the dish again, if I would ever taste the umami flavor bursting through my mother's migas or feel the warmth of a midday "caldo de res." It was too many things hitting me all at once. I just had to suppress them all because it was getting late, and I needed to pack because soon enough, we would be heading out . . . to somewhere.

Please, take a moment to sit back, close your eyes, and play a little game of imagination.

A beat up '55 Chevrolet driven by a man who may be named Chuy. . . Jesus? I'm not really sure. Four boys. Three men. One woman. Two plates of sixty meat tacos. We barely had meat, it was expensive. A bunch of bananas, and a couple hundred miles to go.

There was no money to stop at a restaurant along the way, no time to truly stop and rest. The only thing pushing us along was not our hunger for something other than tacos, but a life we had only seen lived by other people. It was a total of four days from Sabinas to Waukegan, Illinois. Four days of half our party sleeping in the car and the other finding comfort in dirt beds and grass-stained covers because there was simply no space for all of us.

Upon arrival, there was no sun-kissed welcome, but rather a stunned frosted smirk stating, "This is home."

We arrived in the dead of winter. Actually, let me reiterate that, a winter with snow—up until this point we had never seen snow, or really understood what cold really was.

A couple, whom I will never forget, welcomed us into their home. Let us call their basement a refuge where we could finally relax and feel a little safety descend upon our heavy shoulders.

This continued until my father came for us. He was previously in Detroit, Michigan, but had moved down to Chicago because he was offered a better position within a foundation that at the time was called "National Debt." As that was all occurring, we quickly began accommodating ourselves to attempt and return to whatever "normal" we could find.

At the time, I was around ten, and my oldest brother was in his late teens, possibly early twenties, and I remember struggling so much just to learn the basic forms of communication. I was lucky. I was still young, so I had time. I initially started going to school—and a private catholic school at that. My mother was a strong believer behind discipline and knew that public school was not going to grant the outcomes she intended for her sons.

So, while I was able to start in Catholic school, my other brother started working right away. Yes, it's easier when a kid arrives when he's young, about four or five years old, but getting here at ten was still quite difficult—but not impossible.

I remember moments where I would need to answer a question for a nun, and I had to improvise my way through answers because they would slip through my mind. It was tough being a kid stripped of home, attempting to become better for his hardworking parents, and who was constantly reminded of that when I would visit my mother every day at lunch (she was the lunch lady). Yes, my mother worked for my school for free, sort of. Basically, the deal was that her labor would pay for her son's education. So there it was again, sacrifice taking over my mother's spirit—and she did it with a smile.

If this is the land of opportunity, of the "American dream" than you must understand that you do not just receive the American dream. It is not a right, but a privilege. The American dream is received based upon your demeanor, who you are, and how you decide to adjust to the world around you.

My brothers and I have served in the Army, have gone through our own hells and have survived to tell our stories. From receiving from passed down jobs from my older brother like an old worn out sweater that aided in getting me to the next to step, to working at the same job for the last fifty years before opening my own restaurant. All of this topped off with having my own restaurant burn down to the ground and feeling my blood, sweat, and tears dissipate with it.

I have constantly grown through each struggle and have realized that it's the people who aid you on your journey who matter the most.

My wife, for example, who is not just a caretaker for my beautiful children, but has managed to master both roles of mother and father. Whoever said being a wife, a woman, or a mother is a life of bliss is blinded by ignorance. It is only through her constantly motivating and supporting our family that I—that we—are where we are today. It is the work of all of the people who have helped run and put my business where it is today—because a boss or an owner is nothing without his employees. It's for all those people who have worked hard to make my dreams a reality.

This is for every client who's had enough courage to try my food and fall in love with it, and, even more importantly, who have stuck around during the death of my first restaurant, and its rebirth. It is for my children, who I apologize for not spending more time with, obsessed with providing a lifestyle much different than my own while forgetting that there's not enough pay to buy back time we lost.

This is for everyone who feels like nothing is all they'll ever have. To each of you, I leave this question to consider: If diamonds are just glorified pebbles, then who's to say you're not a mine full of jewels?

CALDO DE RES
By Daniel Gutiérrez

Falta nombre del platillo
1.5 – 2 lbs. bone-in beef short ribs (about 4 ribs)
1 cob corn, peeled and cut into quarters
2 carrots, peeled and sliced into chunks
2 pieces of celery sliced into chunks
1 tablespoon olive oil
1/4 yellow onion, sliced thin
1 tomato, chopped
1/4 cup cilantro leaves, plus more for serving
1/2 green cabbage, sliced into two or three wedges
2 white potatoes, scrubbed and sliced into chunks
2 summer squash, sliced into chunks
Salt, to taste
Fresh cilantro, for serving
Lemon or lime wedges, for serving
Sliced fresh jalapeños, for serving
Corn tortillas, for serving

1. Put your meat in a small stock pot.

2. Put 1 gallon of water 2 tablespoons of salt, your onions, tomatoes and 3 garlic cloves.

3. Cook your meat to 3/4 then add all of your ingredients.

4. Let it cook until your meat is done along with your vegetables and it's ready to serve.

WALDO GARCÍA
Riccardo's

17
Purpose

I've come to terms with the fact that I was meant to live the childhood that I did. Looking back on it now, not many can say they could endure that life, but I did. Life has handed me tough times and moments where I've questioned my purpose—to the point where I have felt both unsure and incapable.

Now, this may seem like something ordinary, something that just comes as a surprise bonus inside the gift of life when it's shipped to your front door. It's easy to believe that everyone is granted this, but through time and age, I've come to realize it's not. It's a gift, and I'm glad I received it.

I was raised in a home where my father was not really present. A monthly check titled "missing you" and 500 kisses were the only thing that proved I still had a father. It's not that I say that with anger toward him. At the end of the day, he did it because he loved us. He worked hundreds of miles away from his family and loved ones to maintain something he didn't even get to witness.

It wasn't as if he was completely absent. He did have his occasional visits, of course. They mainly consisted of work, but they brought about some of the most memorable experiences. For instance, the moment I was left for dead.

I was a young kid trying to keep up with my dad, helping as much as I could—almost as if my manhood was being put to the test, and if that was what needed to be done to enjoy any morsel of time with him, then that's what would be done. Well, it either was that my excitement blinded me, or I don't know what was going through my head, but I was sent to go fetch the cattle and instead came back very empty handed. I actually didn't come back at all. At some point in my trip, I didn't recognize the path anymore. The sky came across as unfamiliar, and something told me I wasn't in Kansas anymore (if you didn't catch that, it's a joke I was still in Mexico—I wasn't that lost!) I did however end up lost in a mountain with nowhere to turn and no way to ask for help.

I wish I could tell you this was just a quick detour, a slight bump in the road, but this was no wrong turn; it was again . . . a mountain. After a day, I was lucky enough to come across a home and—this makes me even luckier—it was a couple who invited me to stay with them for the time being until someone came looking for me. My stay lasted three days until my brother and uncle finally found me. Well, I think the main thing I was thankful for was the fact that they were still looking considering that in their minds there was no way I could have survived all those days by myself, enduring God knows what. Now, it's not to say that this is my favorite memory with my father, but when there's only so many times in a year you get to—not only acknowledge his existence, but be part of it—well, you hold on to every memory just a bit tighter and just a bit longer than usual.

Now, because of that, my mother was no longer just "Mom," she was Dad when she turned her back, Dad when she reprimanded us for the mistakes that follow a child's path to life, and Dad when her sweat turned into tears, and she could no longer take being two people at once—like an unavoidable identity crisis she swore she could endure.

There was only so much she could take until her own personal brand of humor and tragedy mask would shatter, returning every morning to again put on her weary face, determined to get through just one more day.

I imagine the difficulty my mother faced as she raised all her children while trying to provide them with everything without the resources to do so. Her creativity to push on astounded me as she hand-made artisan cloths and goods to sell just to keep us afloat.

It hurts being in a situation like that, where you're afraid to ask for life necessities while knowing what the work entails. I remember a part of the reason why I stopped going to school was the constant confrontation that arose with my mother because school was just being school. Well, I can understand her frustration when it seemed like every day I would need something new. At first, it would be supplies, then it stemmed to new books, shoes, clothes, fees, etc. It would all feel like a giant load that I was inadvertently shoving down my mother's throat that was unintentional, but somehow, she would assume it was all on me—as if I enjoyed watching her eyes dim when she realized the subject of our conversation.

It was the same look she gave me when I decided at the age of fifteen to start a new life in the United States. It was a mixture of sadness and doubt, mostly derived from the fact that my mother thought that I would be too lazy to survive out here, knowing the amount of work that I would need to put in. Don't get me wrong, I would have loved to have continued my education, to get a degree, establish myself as a professional, and possibly be in a much different situation than I'm in now. Only one of us, my sister, has been granted that. I'm glad because she is doing well, but at the time, there was my eldest brother, who has unfortunately passed, and another who was making his way in the states—plus my father as well. In the long run, it seemed like a much better possibility than what I was faced with at the time.

My journey began in my hometown of Guanajuato, Mexico, and then into Tijuana, and ended in the states, and I promise it was much longer and difficult than the few words I used to describe it above.

The only reason I can't complain about the experience is because of the people who helped me through it.

It's thanks to people like Ricardo, a man in my hometown who basically took me in as his son, who not only was the person who gave me my first job at a local cleaners, but who also played the role of second father for me. He was a man who taught me right from wrong and showed me about life and how to work. It was thanks to one of my bosses, Adolfo, who gave me an opportunity when I arrived, starting me off as a bus boy and later seeing my potential and moving me into the kitchen.

It was in the kitchen that I learned what I know about food today. It was through my hard work that I gained the knowledge that has helped earn the successes of today. It was because of that, that I found my purpose in life.

Along with the good always comes the bad, and along with that, something that I always try to teach to my children and others is that you always know the right from the wrong and you always have the opportunity to choose between the two. There's always going to be moments and people who prey on your weaknesses, findling them in everything. Like working eighty hours and getting paid for forty, or having a language barrier nailed around you leaving you oblivious to your surroundings, and the worst thing: those same people know that there's nothing you can do. There is no protection on your behalf because the one thing they have against you is what will ruin you. At that point, people have access to your future, they hold the power to determine where your life is going, and there's a long history of failures that only serve as proof to what power in the wrong hands produces.

It was things like receiving an $80 work check for seven days of full-time pay and having to accept it that made me regret my decision of leaving my job which was paying me more in Mexico. It was my brother's constant push to look towards the future and asking me to just hold on another day that made me stay, and it was one of the greatest things this country has granted me that helped make me who I am today: my wife.

When I finally decided to open my restaurant, it was alongside my wife. It was a passing thought like, "Hey, I would love to have this. Maybe it'd be nice to have a small - " Well, as we were both working at the time, our "this" just stayed a thought at the back of our minds as an easy form of conversation. It wasn't until it became the "this" where I would work the kitchen and my wife would work the front of the house trying to make ends meet. And it wasn't until our "secret dream" turned into the restaurant that's had TV debuts, served various famous people, and has received awards, and titles such as, "Restaurant of the Month."

It's because of all of "this" that I can testify to the good and the bad. There are things to fix in the place where we live, just like in any other.

This country has granted me so many gifts, but it's only because I've received so many hardships along the way that I've been able to recognize them and acknowledge what's broken.

What I'm speaking of here is the discrimination toward immigrants and the ignorance that fuels it. The "talk-with-no-action" persona many Americans convey. You hear so many people talking about immigrants who are taking their jobs while they refuse to take the jobs that are available, and it's because they are Americans, and they want to be picky and have the right to be picky. Nobody wants to get paid bare minimum with no benefits to do jobs nobody wants to do. People want good jobs with good pay, and, of course, that is fine. Everyone should feel that way. Americans are automatically born with rights some people may never receive. So, yes, they have the right to not settle. They have the right to earn good money. They have the right to enjoy the freedoms that the United States has to offer, and they have the right to see their dreams become reality.

And I say that with all the love I have for this country. It's granted me the foundation that has allowed for my business to prosper. It has granted my beautiful family opportunities I may have never been able to provide them with in Mexico. It has enabled my son to become independent through amazing education and support he is given within his school, and it has allowed me to discover the boundaries a human is able to break down just when you think your will is not strong enough. It is because of things like that, that I have all of "this."

CHICKEN VESUVIO

By Waldo García

Chicken Vesuvio
2-4 tablespoons olive oil
2 whole chicken cut into serving sizes pieces
4 medium potatoes, cut into quarters lengthwise
2 cloves garlic, crushed and chopped
½ teaspoon of dried oregano
salt and pepper to taste
¼ cup of white wine
2 tablespoons or more chicken stock

1. Preheat oven 350 degrees.

2. Place olive oil in a large skillet and heat until mist rises from the pan.

3. Add Chicken pieces and brown on one side for 10 min. You may have to do this twice or more to do all the chicken, so use more olive oil.

4. Add potatoes and cook until browned.

5. Place pan in oven and bake for 20-30 min minutes or until nicely browned.

6. Remove pan from oven and pour off oil.

7. Add garlic, oregano, salt and pepper.

8. Sauté until garlic is browned.

9. Add wine and swirl until pan is deglazed.

10. Cook until wine is reduced by half.

11. Add chicken stock, bring to boil and serve at once.

If you want a juicier dish, add more stock.

MIGUEL GONZÁLEZ

Los Comales Restaurant in Joliet & 18th Street

—

18
Vision

Have you ever played with wet sand? Gone to the beach and dug a ditch by the seashore neighboring the tide, watching the water as it goes in and out and in and just waited for all the sea foam to gently fall into the hole you've dug where it can rest and be absorbed by every grain of sand? Have you done that? Have you ever taken all that sand and created a structured putty and then used it to construct and build the foundation for anything your mind imagined? What did you build? Was it a tower, was it a mermaid, an igloo . . . a home?

Now, besides building a home, did you ever try living in it? Did you ever imagine the idea of having raw, fragile walls as protection or opening the front door and having chips of your construction bump your head? What if I told you that all this was possible, that you could live in a house made basically of mud… or in my case, clay? What if I told you my home, where I lived day in and day out, was built with the same materials as most children's art projects?

I'm not complaining. It was a humble little home made from the earth for people of the earth and represented who I was and how my family of nine struggling to keep going in life. Resources were limited, and we didn't have what we always needed or wanted, but we always managed to make enough.

I grew up in a little ranch in Jalisco, Mexico. A ranch that probably isn't your top hit on a Google flight search, but to me it was home—a home that I knew couldn't be mine forever.

Then one day one of my family members pushed my siblings and I (basically my whole family) to move to the city of Mexico to look for better opportunities because he knew that where we were, the only possibility was to stay stagnant.

We finally listened, and with that, my siblings and I all migrated to the city of Mexico, leaving my parents behind in the ranch because I guess a part of them couldn't leave the mud hut they had built. Once arriving, food was exactly what we wanted. A brother-in-law had local food posts that were spread all over the city. It was your typical street food . . . but better. I started helping them out and working with them. And quickly, I learned about the preparation of food and what it takes to sell it and how to react to customers. After some time, a brother and I convinced my parents to migrate to the city so we could all be together again.

Time passed, and we enjoyed being together, but it didn't last long because we actually decided that we didn't just want to move from ranch to city; we wanted to move from city to country to new life to new possibilities. So, we embarked on a journey, much like others, crossing what we call the "Big Lake" and arriving in a country that, at that time, didn't receive a lot of people like us. It was difficult arriving in a country where the language was not like ours, the weather wasn't anything like we've experience before, and the first thing you had to do was look for a job because there was no other choice, unless you wanted to end up dead on the street corner or fighting for your life to go back home.

I wasn't picky when it came to work either. Anywhere I could find that they needed me, I went. I started off on a ranch that—to this day, I can't even tell you where it was located—but I did everything I could there: taking care of the horses, cleaning stables, in a sense keeping the place running. It wasn't a career nor a life of choice, but it was a life of a necessity. An inner instinct of survival that didn't waste time on complaining about my misfortunes because they were petty causes compared to the real motivation behind our struggle.

Every time I felt as if life was catching up to me or my seams were at the brink of bursting, I closed my eyes and imagined what I was working for.

I remembered the reason I trudged through inches and inches of snow, carried my days with little to no sleep, and faced every day with a brave face and fearful heart; it was because of them. It was because of my younger brothers who didn't accompany us on our great journey of migration. It was because of them—those who were living in a less than perfect economic situation with an uncertainty for their future. It was because of them, the people who now desperately clung to our existence and confused our names with hope because of a promise we had made to push us all along. All I needed to do was to close my eyes and think of them, of my parents, and suddenly the headache of working two jobs seemed minimal in comparison.

When we first arrived, it was in the house of a brother who had migrated to the United States beforehand. It was nice having someone in the beginning, I will admit, and also having a place to live—which helped to take a huge load off our shoulders—but he could only have us for so long. So in a moment's notice, it seemed like my issues only kept adding up instead of being cut down. In those moments of pure survival, you learn to be savvy with life. It now became a matter of figuring out how we were going to find an apartment or pay our bills or afford furnishing the home god, and on top of it we still had to eat. And then, sometimes you learned how to play a very tough game of eeny- meeny-miny-moe to decide what was really needed because some weeks the pay just wouldn't cut it.

Although it seems bad, that wasn't really the worst of it. The hard part was living without them. Waking up and not hearing my mother's voice. Not hearing one of their famous sayings on respect or humility. I worried about how my parents were doing and keeping up. I thought about everything, not just there, but here too. Knowing that the next day I would have to go back to work playing a hot game of charades just to get by—trying to retain the meaning of each foreign word, but after time being convinced that it was no use. I had so many negative emotions and no one to share them with because even though I had brothers here, there are some things that a person chooses to deal with on their own. And it's not as if they weren't going through the same whirlwind of feelings. So why would I dump mine on them?

Time went by, and through that time came adaptation. I started my own life where I was. I met my wife who has not only been my partner in life but my partner in business. We shared a common bond in need and survived working for other people when we both had visions of our own.

A vision that not only consisted of us moving forward but doing it with things that we knew and love that still retained the essence of who we were.

So now it's been approximately twenty-eight years, but we started our hobby of charreria which is a very famous and boasted tradition in Mexico. We made our own team and competed all over. I could see it finally coming together—our dreams and lives, until one day we surpassed all of the hardships we had faced. It brought me even more joy seeing it in her eyes because I know how much this meant to her. I could see the empty hole in her heart slightly fade. I saw a little girl who lost her father, who became a woman much too soon in order to take care of her younger sister, mask all of her pain and reach for happiness.

Yet, this woman who had all the right to hate life and to question its intentions and doubt in its word became my support system. It's as if after being dragged through the sand, she emerged brand new, like the rising of a phoenix— beautiful against all the disaster. She went through life with some missing pieces, some in the process of mending, and others so vacant and forgotten even time couldn't salvage. Yet, this woman-my wife- does everything in her power so that our family does not end up like her own. She's made it her mission to change the dynamic.

She strives to be the super glue that bonds us as one because it only takes one missing piece to collapse a foundation. She is the type of person who needs to work on depending on others once in a while, but I guess after a whole life of only counting on yourself as a reliable source, the habits become hard to break. Habits like learning how to "live" on your own and not only that, but becoming in charge of someone else's life as well. She reminds me of the strength the worst brings out of you—the humility and selflessness that pain brings out when you don't think you can be broken down anymore, and the resilience against hard times knowing that one way or another, nothing stands a chance when we're together.

It's because of her that this dream even exists because in every step, she was there from beginning to end. It's never been just me or just her. It has been the perfect fusion of us that kick-started the beginning of right now.

The charreria was our first business venture, and for some time I thought it was our only one, until my wife came to me with an idea. She had seen that after service at a very busy church everyone would just leave. There was no place for anyone to eat nearby or to continue their Sunday. My wife didn't just see it as an issue, she saw it as a possibility. She came to me and discussed the idea, and after visiting the place and analyzing the situation, I agreed, and so our first restaurant was born. It's a restaurant that has luckily stood through the test of time, and something that we are so proud of. It's not just a job for us, but a vital factor of our family structure.

We have been lucky enough to create something that has become an icon of our community and has progressed into more than just a small shop. It's the physical representation—each one of them—of the greatness of God and the will to survive.

It reminds me every day of everything I faced, of every moment I felt like breaking down, and it makes me smile in gratitude because I didn't. I was able to do everything I thought I couldn't and so much more alongside my wife.

This restaurant demonstrates a passion for food and determination for success. This restaurant isn't just the story of a lonely young boy working to make ends meet but the story of a young girl that chose to rise from the ashes and turn pain and loneliness into independence and bravery. This restaurant and every plate of food it produces is a little piece of us, not just as a couple, but a family.

SPINE MOLE WITH NOPALITOS

By Miguel González

3 lb. pork backbone (square)
1 lb of cactus (nopalitos)
8 ounces maseca or wheat flour
20 Guajillos chilies
10 puya chiles
1 onion
2 red tomatoes
2 tomatillos

1.Put your meat to cook in a pot and add water until the meat is covered, put 1 1/2 tablespoon of salt and 2 cloves of garlic.

2. Separately sauté the chilies, tomatoes and onion in a little oil.

3. Grind them in the blender put 2 nails with a little juice of the same meat.

4. In another casserole put your nopalitos to cook, after cooked, strain them.

5. In another caserola, put your maseca or wheat flour to cook, mixing constantly until obtaining a semi-golden color (do not neglect your flour, because you can ruin your mole)

6. As soon as your maseca or flour is ready, add the ground ingredients, and continue to move them to avoid mass lumps.

7. Add more broth if necessary so that the mole is not too thick. Add your meat and let it boil for few minutes while continue to stir.

DOLORES HERRERA

Gorditas Don Ángel & Gorditas Lolis

19
Determination

One of the biggest gifts I was granted in this life was an amazing mother who, with her hands, passed down the seedling to what has now boomed into my life. "Gorditas Don Angel" is a story that has yet to end. It started with a woman—my mother—who never wanted to just be nothing in life, who saw necessity within her family, who knew that her husband needed help and didn't just talk about doing something. She did it.

When my mother started making her famous gorditas it was because she herself fell in love with her first taste. Then, it expanded to neighbors and other people within the neighborhood who started lining up just to buy orders of her food. Soon enough, my mother got her own little stand, and it was official: Her gorditas became immortal.

Now, here's where I come in.

All of the kids in the family, 12 to be exact, helped out my mom. When we were on break or after school, our job was to help her with dough or passing them out, and it wasn't just us. This had turned out to be a full-blown family business, and it was nice to see people like her niece helping my mom out too.

So, working with my mom was obviously part of my childhood, but as time went by growing up in small town only helped in increasing my curiosity for the world. The times that I got my fill were when I would head into town to go to school. When I was there, it was like a slightly different world. It was vibrant and full of things that I didn't know there were in the world. More specifically, I mean radio. I remember when I first heard the radio thinking it was the most amazing thing ever, and upon returning home, begged my father for one. Thinking back on it now, I laugh at the naïve and innocent things I would be amused by. But I didn't know any better, and the world to me was just waiting to be discovered.

It wasn't just the little things on the outside, it was what my town had to offer as well that fed into it. Well, more literally, it was my grandmother's chiles pasado that made me feel like the most special girl out there.

I was very loved by my grandparents, and I think it's because I genuinely enjoyed spending time with them. I loved how my grandmother, as soon as she found out I was coming over, would hurry to make my favorite meal. They taught me how to be the person I am today. They emphasized being respectful of what's not yours and to pursue honesty above all things.

My parents and grandparents both left such an impactful mark on my life that I can't imagine being who I am without each of their guidance.

At the end of my high school career, I decided to go to college and pursue a career to become a secretary. Once I finished, I came home and started working for a lawyer who was connected with the church back in town. It was a job that was okay for the moment, and I liked it. But there was something that felt incomplete, like I was looking for something a little more.

It was then that an old friend approached me regarding a shoe store of hers that she was trying to sell. She explained to me the whole story of how she was leaving for the United States and wanted to offer me the store. She made the offer too good to be true. She offered to sell me her merchandise at a discounted rate, made the shoe store sound like a great investment, and even promised that whenever I needed help, she could help find me any extra distributors that I would need.

The offer was tempting, and it gave me a lot to think about, but I wanted to make sure I was making the right choice here. I went back home and mentioned the idea to my dad. I figured that if I was going to consult anybody on this future business venture, it would be him. You know, the one who's worked all of his life and has found business in tending to his animals. I figured that if he gave me the okay, I would finally feel assured with my choice.

Although I was looking for the okay because I liked the idea, I wasn't completely convinced my dad would agree, but when he told me he thought it was a good idea, I knew at that moment that my course had just changed.

My friend—the one who sold me the shoe store—was an impressive business woman. She sought out her prey, pinned it down, and left. She made the whole process simple and easy. She sold me each pair for "x" amount of dollars so that I would have some sort of inventory when I started. I felt nervous yet elated as the lady wished me good luck and went on her way. I quickly organized my shop and got ready because opening was coming soon.

Well, you remember that moment of happiness that came over me? Well, it came and left very quickly after my first day. There I was, happy go lucky, running around my business attending to my customers when one of them asked for the other shoe to the pair. I happily obliged running to the back room when something felt a bit off. When I went to grab the box, I noticed it felt a lot lighter than it should, almost as if it were empty. Well, I opened it, and it was empty, so I went to check another box, convincing myself it was probably a misplaced shoe. I reached for the next box not thinking much of the situation, until yet again, it felt … empty. Now, I was beginning to panic. I grabbed another and another and another, and it felt like forever until I realized that they were all empty. Well, not empty, but they only held one shoe so, to me, they might as well have been empty because they were leaving me with nothing.

I couldn't believe that this woman who had promised me so much left me with a run-down business, and I was the one who fell for it.

I won't lie. That situation tore me down, but I continued my shoe store for two years afterwards, with the help of my dad who took me out to buy merchandise every other week. But after two years, I decided to leave the business because I simply didn't want to do it anymore.

My life after that kind of ran on impulse, and when I was 18, I felt the sudden urge to move to the United States. I didn't really have an exact reason for wanting to leave; it was as if all of those years of wondering and questioning what was out there finally caught up to me. I wanted to venture outside of the realm that I called home, outside the little town that I was from, and see what else the world had to offer. My mom wasn't for it. She was upset about my infatuation with leaving. She didn't quite understand why I needed to leave. I think a part of her maybe even started questioning what could've been better to make me stay, but none of it was her fault. There was really nothing that she could do at that point to make me stay because I had already made up my mind.

When I finally decided to leave, I arrived in California—at the house of one of my cousins to be exact. She was kind enough to lend me her home, give me a room and a bed to sleep in, and, along with her husband, we would go on the weekends to collect aluminum to later sell to companies. It wasn't a vacation per se, but I can remember so many things about my trip that were so different than back home.

I know that my cousins thought that I was the funniest girl out there because of the fact that I got so excited with the unknown. I remember one time we went to a major store like Kmart, a store where my cousin parked farther away from the doors, and we had to enter the store for food slowly, fearful immigration would catch us. I can remember her telling me to be quiet and to act relaxed, that I couldn't act surprised over each new gadget that I found, that I had to act like I was used to it. Well, I tried, I really did, and it was all going fine until we reached the door and it slid open . . . you know, because it was automatic. Well, not only did it startle me, but I did a slight look to each side to make sure the coast was clear and as soon as I felt safe I yelled like I never yelled before. It was the oddest thing to think that these doors knew you were coming—that the sense of you was enough for them to open—and I know even talking about it now how silly it seems, but back then, it was as if I was a pirate constantly discovering new treasures, and I think that's how life should be.

You should never just be content with what you have; you should feed your curiosity, let it take you where it wants to, and every day feel as if you're finding new treasures.

I know right now it seems like my trip was pretty easy breezy, but it wasn't that simple. Besides being an amazing time, I also know that there's a part of me that wishes she would've listen to her parents just a little bit more because on top of all the values and gifts they gave me, there's something I just didn't follow.

By the time I arrived in the United States, I had one child. When I moved here, I met the man who would soon become fatther to my youngest two children—a man who accompanied me through various rough times in my life. I'll never forget the day I was at home relaxing. I was with my family when I got a call from one of my sisters telling me that if I wanted to see my mom that I needed to come now before it was too late. So, my family and I packed our bags and went to spend our last few days with my mother. I think it was a rough time for all of the family—brought together again, but for all the wrong reasons. I think the wind felt colder that night too, and it seemed as if the whole earth wished it was a happier occassion. I returned back home with a new hunger in mind, a hunger to be something more.

I opened up a little shack outside of the Coca-Cola Company. At the time, Coca-Cola was nice enough to offer you a little post, give you a spot to set up your things, and what else could I do but sell but my mother's food? It was the one thing that I knew, and knew well. I remembered watching her toss the dough as a child, and as I do it even today, I can feel her watching over me, laughing with me when things go right and when things go wrong. I spent a long time outside of the Coca-Cola Company when eventually my business got too big. There was a woman who offered me her garage that was directly in front of the company. To this day, I'm so thankful to them for opening their place for me, a place where I had a space for tables and for accommodating people. It was a good few years, but I lost it. Finally, I had to leave and was pushed to open my new restaurant. It was the right thing to do. It's a restaurant that not only serves food, but joy. It was because of that food that I was able to build our house, the house I always joked is made from gorditas. It's hard work that brought me along to where I am now. I don't ever want to come across like this is mine because I take no credit for it. I give it all to my mother and the love she taught my hands and left in my stomach.

ENCHILADAS

By Dolores Herrera

Santiago Papasquiaro Durango Style

Sauce
12 Chiles Red Anchos
2 tablets of Chocolate Abuelita
4 ounces of sugar
1 large stick of cinnamon
3 cloves
½ teaspoon of salt
3 ounces unsalted peanut

Filling
Chihuahua or your favorite shredded cheese
1 finely chopped onion
24 tortillas
2 cups frying oil

1. Soak the seedless chile in hot water until its soft.

2. Using a blender, mix the chile with the rest of the ingredients, chocolate, sugar, cinnamon, cloves, salt, unsalted peanuts.

3. Blend and fry in a frying pan with 2 ounces of oil. Let it boil for 3 minutes while stirring.

4. In another hot pan, put the rest of the oil and pass the previously heated tortillas one by one, submerging in the sauce and spreading on the plate, where they are filled with cheese and chopped onion.

5. Cover the tortilla with another, equally submerged in sauce and served.

DAVID CASTELAN

Autentico Burrito Restaurant

20
A Last Story About the Man I Did Not Know

There's this man that I know, quite well actually, who tells me stories that he thinks I don't listen to, makes faces at me when he thinks I'm not looking, and teaches me things he thinks I don't care for—but he does it anyway. This is a testimony of all of those things he's convinced I know nothing about.

This man has taught me about hard work, and I mean really hard work. He has humbled me even before an ego could even form inside of me and has denied me the ability of being spoiled even more than the gift of being an American readily gives. Born and bred in the small town of Trojes, Mexico, he was one of thirteen children—eight of whom survived. He grew up in a home that would only appear on a HGTV special edition where they show a cute couple flipping homes that most would mistake for a mud pile. He had a mother who never taught him to think of women as weak because a simple look would let him know to tone it down before she proved it to him.

Through an unfortunate turn of events, he had a father who was among the most intelligent and savviest businessmen in town. The only downside seemed to be that all his business seemed to only benefit his love for booze and nights at bars. It seemed like all of his businesses led him to big talk that left him owing something to everyone in town, and that pressure only impacted his family. His abuse was not just toward liquor, but toward the people he was supposed to love and take care of as well.

He will either tell you stories about how great his life was or how easy I have it. He will tell you of how the best times he had were playing soccer with his brothers and other local kids on dirt roads and dusty empty plots of lands. He'll tell you about having crowds of kids watching and placing bets on intense matches of marbles during recess. He might even tell you about the acre of land filled with tomato plants his uncle gifted him and how he harvested and cared for all of it himself. He also won't fail to mention how he wore the same shoes for months on end, that when he kicked the ball and a strap went loose, it only meant he had to find a more creative way to make it last just a little longer.

He'll mention that he got really good at marbles because it was the only chance his brothers and he would have at affording lunch that day. He most definitely won't forget to say that his tomato plants were basically deemed worthless and couldn't even make a quick buck out of them because they all went bad. He'll tell you all of this and more and still brag that the river where their clothes were washed is the best of them all, that the fruit trees provided the best snacks, and the scenery of his state is above par as it is easily the best in all the country.

He'll tell you all of this and more, and I bet he thinks I didn't know.

This man left all of his bragging rights at the age of fourteen, arriving in the country he now calls home. The only thing he had was a Spanish vocabulary, a couple of siblings who had arrived here before him, and a whole lot of work laid out ahead of him. There was a sense of guidance that a young man still needs that he was left to figure out on his own. This man fell into vices that he later had to fall out of, but there was no one there to save him the trip.

This man knows a thing or two about world class dining. He's had a job at just about any type of restaurant one can imagine—American, Japanese, Greek, and Mexican. You name it, and I'm sure this man will somehow know something about it, but I bet you this man will not think that I know.

This man refused to allow his life to be a waste and recognized that he would have to be the one who opened the doors for him. Luckily for him, there was no, "Ingles sin Barreras" at his disposal. Actually, there were a lot of "barreras" between him and it, but at the speed of ten words a day, he tore them down. Oh, right, you might not know of the infamous "ten words a day." Well, this man committed himself to learning ten new words a day in English and utilizing them throughout the next day in order to forge the gap that often gets ignored between languages.

This man decided that he would take the humiliation that came attached with incorrect pronunciation and botched use of meaning, so that one day he himself could tell you his story.

This man taught me that there is no point in saying you want things if you're not willing to work for them. He taught me that the only person who has control of your life is you, so why would you allow yourself to be content with just being adequate?

I bet you this man thinks that I do not care about things like this.

This man has a love story . . . well, one of many for this man. He has some charm to his name, but there is only one story that truly counts. It's the one about the beautiful waitress who took his heart and never gave it back, as much as she desperately tried to in the beginning. True to his character, this man was convinced his heart was never his but hers to begin with. This man, through many moments of persistence, made the beautiful waitress his wife and swore he would do everything in his will to provide her with everything she deserved and more and when the woman had their first daughter, he swore it to her too.

This man had a wife and a child, two jobs and classes to attend, no car, but a nice pair of legs. A nice pair of legs adorned in the finest garments only a local thrift store could provide. Those legs withstood blizzards, thunderstorms, floods and more, but, of course, the man was protected in permeable $2.99 polyester and nothing could get through his thick skin. This man would get four hours of sleep just so he could go to culinary school, work, and do it all over again. This man turned down an amazing position with a massive company as an executive chef just so he could get a certificate that said, "Yes, you really did it."

This man has taught me all about sacrifice, about what it really takes to get the things that you want, but I bet you this man thinks that I do not care.

Lastly, this man moved his family from a rented closet—I mean a room—to an actual home at the age of twenty-two. That's also the age when the man finally began to fulfill his promise. This man opened his first restaurant. It was a tiny place. It did its job and served its purpose, but it was the man's dream coming to life and this man could not be happier. The man served food that only his upbringing taught him using the skills his schooling had supplied. Soon, there were moments when this man just sat back in awe, pinching himself as he saw his restaurant full of smiling people eating and enjoying his food. It was as if this man had finally done something right, but there's something about other people's success that doesn't seem to sit quite well with some people. It's because of this that the man learned that people do not always reciprocate with what they are given, and that no one, and that does mean no one—not your friends, family, or anyone—is too good or above anything.

It's the people that this man helped the most who sabotaged and betrayed the one thing he spent all of his life working towards. It was in a moment like this that the man learned that life is tough, and it forces you to be tougher.

It is true. I have learned this lesson from this man. But he does not know I know.

This man has since expanded beyond his restaurants into one of the most renowned ice cream franchises in all of Mexico and successfully brought his business into the states. This man has learned about success in abundance, and it has not only come in monetary form, but in the things you may think are just part of life. This man has been married to his beautiful wife for over fifteen years, is blessed with three children (two other separate furry babies whom the children may have begged for, but that is beside the point), and at one point, when he truly felt lost, found a home in a church where he finally found God. This man has realized that there is no point in having riches if you cannot enjoy them, and sometimes the biggest riches you have are in the simple joys life has already granted you.

This man is not weak. Actually, it may be the last word to describe him. The one time I actually saw this man cry, I briefly felt as if I was transported into a different land because I genuinely believed he was incapable of producing tears. If you see this man, you will know exactly why that assumption was made, but I have seen this man attempt to maintain a facade where everything is okay, so much so that sometimes I would like to tell him that it's okay for things to not be okay—that I know sometimes life gets a little too hard for even him to handle. I would tell him that I know when the bills come in, and I don't just think about the ones that come distributed by the mailman to the white picket fence home he's provided us with, but the ones that come from every business. That I hate the amount of times his phone rings just as much or even more than he does because it seems like a short game of Russian roulette. Either he gets the empty shot where his wife is calling or the bullet when yet again something goes wrong, and inevitably it seems as if he is the only one who is able to fix it. That I see when he stays sitting in his pickup truck right outside our door just a little longer than usual attempting to suppress his emotions like when you hold a bursting balloon by its mouth slowly letting the wind out of it.

I'd like to tell him that I see when he worries, even more when he's mad, rarely when he's sad, and many times when he laughs at jokes that only he thinks are funny, but sometimes I laugh anyways.

I'd like to tell this man that I know he stresses over not being able to provide the life he has provided us with. And I'd like to tell the man that it is okay, that I have not just heard his story, but I have listened to it—even though I bet he thinks I never do. I want to tell him that because of the man he is, he has made me the woman I am today. That I've taken the good with the bad, not always joyfully, but I've taken it. I want him to know that, because of him, I know the feeling of pride that spreads over your body when something is achieved because you've worked for it. He taught me you should always seek to learn more, and even when you think you know it all to learn even more, and that it's impossible to survive in this world without thick skin unless you want to get drenched. And it's because of him that I am the most stubborn, driven, unsatisfied, outspoken, and passionate woman you may ever come across.

He doesn't know that these things in my heart and mind, but they are there. They've always been there.

I've learned how to clean up an uprooted tree, run a business, refill steering fluid, so many conspiracies on aliens, and so many other things, but I bet you this man thinks I don't care.

I'd like to tell him there is no point to his facade because his mask has worn down and he has fulfilled his promise. I see when he takes another blow where his wounds have just healed, but I bet you this man thinks I am not looking.

I would like to tell you that this man has a name, David Castelan.

To me, it's Father . . . well, to be frank, it's Daddy, but that seems to take away from the sophisticated essence I was trying to convey. Of course, I am still only eighteen, so maybe we'll just meet half way and go with "Dad."

This man is my dad, and that's pretty cool too.

PART TWO

COMMUNITY LEADERS

ELENA BEATRIZ MELENDEZ

My name is Elena Beatriz Melendez. I am 47 years old. I was born in Tegucigalpa, Honduras, a picturesque country surrounded by mountains and rivers. Closing my eyes, the smell of pine comes to mind and a freshness that remains alive in my memory. Honduras has many lovely customs and traditions. We are full of folklore, ancestral foods and hubbub. We are a happy people for whom dance and music is present from the moment of birth. We are a brave race mixed with indigenous Maya, Spanish, African, and more.

In my memory, I have so many happy anecdotes, just as I have sad ones.

Today, I will speak to you of what helped me succeed and be where I am today. I am owner of a television program in Chicago,

Executive Director of the Central American Festival, founder of the Association of Honduran Culture in Chicago, and founder of the Angels of Love project in Chicago, which focuses on helping children in Honduras. It is my dream to bring this help to all of Central America.

Well . . . everything began with me as a child. I remember the suffering that we had to go through for being a family of very little resources. There were many times when we didn't have anything to eat—going to bed with only a cup of coffee and a tortilla smeared with margarine or pig lard. I am the youngest of 47 siblings, all of whom I love, respect and miss.

As a child, I was very rebellious and mischievous, not understanding that we were SO poor or the reason why others had a means of living comfortably while we did not. My father's love toward me was ever present, but of my mother, I remember little for the first eight years of my life. I grew up in different homes. Some days I was in a house with an aunt, other days in the home of one of my mother's friends. At times I would stay with my godparents . . . such was my childhood.

I could speak with you about many stories that impacted my life, but I believe what held the most influence was seeing the amount of poverty in my country.

Arriving in this country at the age of thirteen, I saw my mother working arduously to help many of our family members, and even friends, working as a tiny ant would to bring us here one by one, and doing it all with happiness and love.

I asked her why once.

Wouldn't it be better to save and put away her money for herself and her old age? She told me she could never be pleased with not knowing she was doing something for those who needed it most.

I could never understand how, despite making so little and paying her offerings toward a pact she made with God, she could still provide my brother and I with Sabbath school—seeing as how we attended the Seventh Day Adventist church. She would take on all of the household needs, and it still baffled me how our refrigerator would always be full.

Our house would always play host to international students who would live with us temporarily, my mother offered these young people a place to stay while they made money for their studies. I also remember and miss those Saturday lunches where our house would be full of young people without families that would come to share in our blessings. We would never be without my mother's delicious rice in our home! She would sauté her rice with onion, garlic and green bell pepper over low heat, allowing it to toast before adding tomato, salt, a chicken bouillon cube, a bit of margarine and finally water. What a delicious rice she would make . . .

And her Honduran red silk beans . . . I close my eyes and I get a waft of that scent of iron they exuded. I go back to that first boiling I can remember, where the house filled with the delicious aroma of beans with garlic, onion, cilantro . . . and I can see my mother—a small woman—happily preparing everything, all while showing her children that giving and sharing is how we receive God's blessings. I think—and I am sure—that this is how my mother, with all of her faults and virtues, went molding the character of this rebellious girl and went placing in my heart the love for helping and serving others.

Although my parents were, like all other human beings, people that made mistakes, they were also people with dignity and honesty. I will bring you another experience that influenced me, formed my character, and gave part to my values.

I do not agree with violence, but many times children need a heavy hand.

As a child of twelve, my father brought me from the country of El Salvador back to Honduras. My father was bringing me back to live in a small house he owned in the outskirts of Tegucigalpa, in a small town named Nueva Aldea. It's a very pretty place, full of fruit trees and pines. There, I was left in the care of a man named Don Mundo. He was surely about a hundred years old because he had wrinkles on top of his wrinkles and he walked SO slowly he must have been competing against tortoises for the title, arriving to the final goal two days later.

This man was good and noble with few like him in the Honduras that I remember. He worried about me and would take care of me as if I were a treasure. And together with my friend Licha, we would play so many pranks on him! He would often appear angry with us, but I'm sure, deep down. he was entertained with our little acts of mischief. He would always offer me advice, and I still have clear memories of all of the stories he would tell.

They say he had been a soldier for the guard of one Mr. Tomas Martinez Caquica. Every time this man would pass by, everyone would feel the fear wash over them. Well, I can still see Don Mundo sitting and regaling me with his orders alongside the feared General. He would always sit with a pole in his hand to write in the dirt floor with. (What he was writing, who knows, because he didn't know how to write!)

Sometimes he would hit the air as if trying to scare away some bad memory. Sometimes he would stare into nothing for short periods of time, which—for me—felt eternal, and I would desperately wait for his return in order to finish his stories. I can see him sitting there, in front of the flickering light of a gas lamp, He was a man of very short stature, his skin a dark indigenous with no teeth, a shirt and pants of manta, sandals and his machete tied to his waist, always giving off the scent of clove and cinnamon. Every time my father would scold me, Don Mundo would tell me I needed to bless and obey him, for it was mandated by God and that it was a sin to judge your parents.

My father almost never scolded me, and, from a young age, I had an influence over him.

I think it was because my mother had the great idea of naming me after my grandmother, Ms. Elena Gutierrez de Melendez. Or perhaps it was because I was born when my father was sixty years old. Well, he was accustomed to arriving on Sunday mornings, carrying the vegetables that weren't on the terrains as well as white bones with pieces of meaty beef to make a soup (that was only delicious when he made it). We call it Honduran beef soup; everyone else calls it beef stew.

As I was telling you, my father would come home every Sunday morning and would leave every Monday morning to go back to Tegucigalpa. I would remain with old Mundo for the rest of the week. We lived on what the land produced there: ayote, mango trees and plum trees, corn, mustard, cashew fruits . . . there was quite the variety of fruits. Because I was so curious, I would try them all. I always liked eating bread and cheese, so Mondays afternoons were my favorite. The baker would come by as well as the man who sold cheese.

I developed a bad habit when my father was sleeping.

My father was accustomed to removing his trousers and hanging them up on the back of the chair. He would lay down to sleep, and I always slept at my father's feet. One day, I got the bright idea of getting up while he was sleeping to take money from his pants. I took one lempira and that week and bought bread and cheese with my friend, Licha. We really enjoyed it. So much so that the following week I went back to do the same. While my father was sleeping, I got up, put my little hand in my father's pants, and took another bill for one lempira.

And so, the weeks went by and, honestly, I don't remember how many weeks it was, but one day I went to put my hand in, and I took out a bill for 100 lempiras. Back in 1982, 100 lempiras was a lot of money!

This particular week, Licha and I ate just about everything. We bought everything we could. We bought meat, I gave away some money, I was like a crazed little girl just sharing with everyone and, well, we even had more than enough to last us for the next week. But at this point, it was already a habit to go into my father's pants, so that next week I went to do it again.

I always waited for my father to be so deep in sleep that he would snore. I went in slowly . . . slowly I put my hand into his pants. I was twelve years old at the time. I put my little hand in his pants and I could feel the bills, my adrenaline rising now that this was becoming something of a thrill for me. I was feeling very pleased as I was removing my hand, when I feel a strong hand grab my arm and say to me, "I GOT YOU!!!!"

"YOU SHAMELESS GIANT THIEF! You'll see what I'm going to do to you now! Surely you will hate me, but in your future—when you're a good woman—you'll thank and bless me!!!"

My father grabbed me and took me from the room, taking me through that path that seemed immense to me. I knew that, while my father never hit me, when he disciplined, it was for something well-deserved, and that it would be a very hard discipline.

He put my hands over the coal in the fire.

The coals were white on the top, but if you blew on them it was obvious that they were burning! They were a pulsing bright red, and, there was where my father put my hands. I gave out a gut- wrenching scream. I looked at him and asked, "Why Daddy?"

He answered, "Because I want to make an honest woman out of you. Because I don't want you to become a thief or a criminal. Today, you are robbing me, your father. Tomorrow, you will rob someone else."

I ran out.

I don't remember what time it was. Perhaps it was nine, ten . . . maybe even eleven o' clock at night. I don't remember what time it was. But I went running to a neighboring woman's house whom we called La Comadre, and I arrived crying, showing her my hands.

In that moment, I hated my father. That man whom I loved so much, the one whose feet I would kiss. That man I admired for whom, in that moment, I felt so much hate and disdain for. Rage! My mind raced to thinking of all the ways I would get revenge, of all the wicked things I could do to make him feel the pain I myself had felt! And I cried and cried.

La Comadre, I recall, put egg yolks and aloe on my hands, but nothing could take away that pain. There was no number of pills that could and, for as many things as they gave me, I ended up falling asleep at the feet of La Comadre, having cried desperately.

That's when I asked myself, "Why mother? Why did you leave me? Why did you abandon me?"

I complained about it and my hate toward my mother grew because she had abandoned me when I was barely nine years old. So that's how time went by for two weeks. I stayed in the house of La Comadre and my father, who loved me, remained attentive to my needs but chose not to seek me out. His reason: to not coddle me in order for me to open my eyes to the lesson of all this.

I look back now at his extreme punishment and my mother leaving me as a child, and there is one key difference.

I am a parent now too.

I now understand the reason for their actions and have an appreciation for their emotional and relative sacrifices that would eventually shape who I am today. Those lessons I learned taught me that both my mother and father suffered too! But, that in the end, it is for the love of humanity and for the caring of others that we must endure distances of all sorts.

This is my story, and these are the experiences that molded that rebellious and curious child into the confident leader I am today.

I consider that the book Beyond the Wall is of the utmost importance during these times, since it reveals with nobleness the richness of our values and traditions where love and sacrifice abound.

QUE LA MÚSICA NUNCA MUERA
(May the Music Never Die)
by Elizabeth Cervantes

I never met my paternal grandfather. Well, I don't recall meeting him would be more accurate. He passed on to a greater life when I was one year old. Neftali Cervantes was his name. The night he died in Zamora, Michoacán, I let out "a loud, sudden cry" my grandmother says. Inconsolable. Like if somehow I knew he was passing on. I like to think that it was because our souls were connected in one special way: through mariachi.

My grandfather Neftali was a trailblazer, he had that in common with my father, Juan. I could argue that my father was the only one of his sons who really took after him. Born in Ixtlán de los Hervores, Michoacán, my grandfather was a trained musician, and formed part of a local town banda—they played the classics. Soon thereafter, my grandfather took up mariachi, I can only guess because of the genre's elegant style and endless possibilities to create music. He trained all his sons and grandsons in this genre, starting with my father with the trumpet at age twelve. By age fourteen, my father was embarking on his first international tour with a youth mariachi group set to perform in major cities across the United States. My grandfather was proud. He formed Mariachi Los Caporales with all his sons eventually—which became the most recognized, talented group in the region. I'm sure this made him even more proud until... he couldn't play anymore.

The age and diabetes had kicked in, and his strength for playing the trumpet just wasn't the same. Still, he went to all of the group's bookings and even dressed in full mariachi attire, as the group's representative—a highly respected one. Artists' managers frequently complimented him on the caliber and musicianship of his group. One can only wonder what leadership qualities he must have possessed to achieve such a place in the music world, to make his group the most loved, most requested, most enjoyed. Not only have that, but to make his sons, grandsons, and great-grandchildren true ambassadors of Mariachi music: a Mexican treasure and official national heritage.

Passion. That's it. I believe passion to be so indescribably powerful in the business of accomplishing your dreams. Sometimes I forget why I'm so passionate about the work I do. And then, I remember. My grandfather. Some days I wish very hard, with all my heart, that I could have met him, grown up next to him. But life has other plans for you sometimes. "El hombre propone y Dios dispone" the bible says. And, my father would often repeat that. Meaning, that you can plan, propose, decide, but ultimately God provides for it or for something entirely different. An idea that rings true for me, for most of my life.

Here I am, almost two-thousand miles away from the land that knew my grandfather, Zamora—home of the indescribable aroma of green chickpeas roasting on the comal in the street, or the sweetness that reaches your nostrils when la señora sets her basket of fresh bread on the plaza ground, the sound of mariachi and banda, and visions of kids playing with their animal shaped balloon-like toys. I feel like I missed out on this sometimes, not growing up in Mexico. And other times, I feel like I can cherish it more now that I have been able to return, precisely because I missed out on it. When I was four years old—after my father had toured the world from Venezuela, to France, Germany, and the U.S., with Mariachi Estampas de Mexico along with the very well-known Ballet Folkloric of Amalia Hernandez,—we left Mexico and permanently moved to Chicago. My mother wanted me to start school in one place and finish there. She was a little bit terrified of having to constantly move me out of school if we had decided to follow my father on his music tours. I was unable to choose growing up near my grandparents and extended family; borders and unjust policies chose for me. It was a done deal. We stayed in Chicago, and I quickly adapted to my new home. Pilsen didn't foreign to different to me. I regularly saw mariachis gathering up on the corner of 18th Street and Blue Island ready to head to a music gig. My father played with Mariachi Guadalajara (the best group of the Chicagoland area in the nineties), and I saw him in his mariachi attire at least four days out of the week.

Music was ever-present in my home, instruments were in every direction you looked, and I had no choice but to end up loving mariachi music. I loved the conversations I had with my father about his music career. He very often talked about how much he missed his dad and how the musician he had become had everything to do with how Neftali Cervantes, the man who trained him, taught him with passion and discipline. He often wished his father was still alive to see my father unfold his dream.

"Cual es tu sueño, apa?" I would ask him. "Que la música de mariachi nunca muera." That mariachi music never dies. "Y como le vas a hacer?" I would follow up. "Enseñándole nuestra música a los niños, como mi jefe me enseño a mi." Teaching music to kids, the way my dad taught me. I'm not sure at what point I knew I wanted to be one forever. A mariachi. Perhaps it was when I first realized my heart would skip a beat when I would hear a guitarrón in harmony with the vihuela (and it happens still every time). Or perhaps it was when I realized what it felt to be in love. The type of love that makes you happy, truly happy— that you can't believe you can feel such a thing. I felt that at age fourteen, when I became the first girl (and the only grand-daughter of Neftali Cervantes) in four generations of mariachi musicians to wear a traditional mariachi suit, pick up the vihuela, and perform with a group. I wished again then that I could have met my grandfather.

Growing up in the United States, as part of an immigrant family, was hard. My siblings and I were our parents' official translators, advocates, and representatives. We learned early on that we would sometimes need to stand up to injustices. Yet, we knew from our parents that this experience would make us into stronger human beings. There is no doubt that this is why I became involved in the fight for immigrant rights. I made it to college, majored in sociology and unexpectedly, began devoting my life and career to community organizing and advocacy. I go to work every day knowing I belong to a community of empowered undocumented families and youth, like myself, that are building power for immigrants in Chicago's southwest suburbs. I wake up some days, and tell myself "what a cool job I have."

Yes, building immigrant power is my real job, and I go at it with passion every day. Well, some days are harder than most. Some days, you think you won't live to see justice in the world. But then, on those hard days, I swing by our after-school youth mariachi program, where my father teaches and directs music. And, I remember that not all is lost in the world. At least, mariachi music isn't. My father devoted his entire life to learning, performing, appreciating, rescuing, and living mariachi music. Almost 50 years. A good number of those years, he performed with some of the most memorable artists Mexico has known. Today, his audience is children—little musicians-in-the-making —who may not have ever experienced the beauty of mariachi music had it not been for my father and the passion he transmits to them when he performs and teaches.

I may not have met my grandfather. Or maybe, I did. Through my father and the legacy of music, passion and resilience he is helping to carry on. And that's what I believe this book is about. Passion. Resilience. Dedication. All values that are such an integral part of immigrant families and weaved into their character and identities. I know what it's like to be assigned to a category of people—the Latino/ Hispanic category, the Mexicans, the "dreamers," the immigrants, and so forth. But there is so much more to my story, like I have shared here, and so much much more to the stories of immigrants than you often get to know. Like for example, what it takes to leave your homeland and venture out to a whole new world. Or the struggle to learn English and be scrutinized for your accent. Or the will and determination you hold onto in order to accomplish your dreams in a country that is not your own, at least at first.

WHO IS ALDERMAN MILLY SANTIAGO?

Milly Santiago was born in Puerto Rico and came to Chicago in the late 70s when she was already an adult. Her story is not any different from the many Latinos and immigrants who come to this country to seek a better life.

Since she came to Chicago, she has always worked in different jobs. She went to college and got a degree in communications and journalism. Santiago started doing radio commercials before being hired as a radio announcer with WOJO and other radio brokers. She never stopped dreaming and wanting to do more.

For close to twenty years, Santiago was the voice of the Latino community in Chicago while working as a news reporter and news anchor for Telemundo and Univision. She was a tireless and aggressive reporter who searched for the truth behind her stories, either on issues related to public education, health or housing, discrimination, immigration issues, politics, breaking news or entertainment.

After living in the 31st Ward for more than thirty years, Milly decided to run for office based on concerns and conversations with people from different walks of life. People saw in Santiago new blood, a voice and someone who could take the destiny of the ward in a different direction. She decided to give it try, especially because politics was something that she always enjoyed.

At that time (2014) Santiago was working for the state government in the area of communications for state agencies. After consulting with close friends and her family, she put a group of people together and strategies to enter the race against someone who had been in office for twenty-four years.

She admits that it was a very difficult race considering her lack of financial resources against someone who had a lot of money and the Democratic machine behind him. She was fearless! Santiago did not allow any negative comments or intimidation to get in her way. She knew the issues and had a positive platform of change and prosperity for the residents of the ward. Her name recognition and track record of social and community involvement were key components to gain the voters' trust. She walked the streets of her ward tirelessly for five years under the brutal winter of 2014-15. She knocked on doors every single day bringing her message of change, of the independent voice she wanted to be and the leader the community desperately needed.

Santiago forced a runoff along with the Mayor of Chicago, for the first time in history. She was declared the winner and was sworn in in May 2015. This is the biggest challenge and accomplishment in her life. That same year, she received the good news that her daughter was having a boy. For Santiago, 2015 marked one of the most important moments in her life. She feels blessed knowing that as the Alderman of the 31st Ward, people are very happy with changes that are happening in the area, including new businesses, more economic development that creates more jobs for the people in the ward, more police presence, a stronger partnership with the schools, Chicago Police Department, community organizations, block clubs and residents in general.

She attributes her success and accomplishments to her parents' example of public service, compassion, humility and integrity. Her parents taught her to care and share with people the moral and family values, the "work hard for what we want in life" thinking and to be the example of good work for future generations.

Santiago lost her dad October of 2016, after a short period of illness. Her loss has been very difficult knowing that her mother is also very ill after suffering a stroke in July of last year. She goes back to Puerto Rico very often to care for her mom and give her sister Tere some days of relief.

The Alderman's best moments are when she gets to spend time with her two-year-old grandson, Enzo. The arrival of that child in her life has made her a completely different woman. She says she could have the worst day or week, but once she gets to hold her grandson in her arms, something magical happens.

Santiago enjoys what she is doing—which is to serve the constituents of her ward. She goes to almost every block party during summertime, attends festivals, church events, and other events that take place in her ward and other parts of the city.

"This is not a part-time job as people think it is. This is a 24/7 job, and I won't do anything else but to serve my residents and be there for them all the time," she says. "I don't know how other aldermen could hold another job or manage a business while being an alderman. For me to be that leader that people need to have, I have to be a full-time alderman."

The best feeling that Alderman Santiago has at the end of the day is good feedback from residents expressing how happy they are that their requests were addressed. When she walks her ward every week, the best reward is when constituents open the door and greet her with a smile and a thank you for taking care of the ward and for being always accessible for them.

Alderman Santiago says her life is fulfilled knowing that she is doing what she enjoys the most—to serve the people and be able to contribute to a better quality of life every day for those she represents.

I believe this book serves as a guide and inspiration for many Latinos to look for that leader we all have inside, but sometimes we have not let it out for different reasons. Our stories can be the reflection of so many men and women who, I am sure, share similar stories. With mine, I urge you to lose your fear, to dream, to set goals and to conquer what is possible—with faith in oneself, tenacity and conviction. Success could have obstacles, but never limits.

ABOUT THE WRITER
ESMERALDA CASTELAN

—

Esmeralda is a young aspiring Latina artist fully devoted to her Hispanic roots and culture. Ever since one can remember Esmeralda could be found with her nose between books or with a mic in hand. Whether it's singing, writing, performing, or volunteering Esmeralda's true passion lies within helping and contributing to other people's happiness. Esmeralda is a true jack of all trades who's original love for music led her to audition for the X factor, The Voice kids, La Banda, and other shows alike. It was when she was 13 she took a passion- that truly was always there just never fully acknowledged- for writing to the next level. Esmeralda began composing her own poetry and later competing with them in statewide, and even nation wide competitions all at the same age. These competitions brought upon multiple opportunities such as being broadcasted on Batavia TV for waterline writers and being a regular performer at the annual Day of the immigrant festival in Bolingbrook, IL. Throughout all of this Esmeralda has maintained a steady sense of humility and kindness along with just a little spunk in her eclectic demeanor. It is because of this strong sense of identity that led Esmeralda to contribute to her mother's idea for the book, "*Beyond the Wall.*" The mother and daughter duo decided they wanted to create something eternal, something that for generations to come could be cherished and referenced, something big that could reach millions and make a change something like a book. They wanted this book to not only shine a light on the beauty of the Latino culture, but to also challenge the false allegations and stereotypes that follow the Latino community. "We wanted to create something that truly shows the beauty of who we are. That we are not malicious or self- indulgent, but rather we are joy and gratitude, colors and flavors, all intertwined into one mesmerizing community who is not separated by these traits but rather unified by our contributions to not just ourselves, but the human race", says Esmeralda. *Beyond the Wall* is a book of acceptance and epiphanies, it's more than a physical object, it's a gift of acceptance and understanding meant to break down borders. It's a book that shouts, "Hope is waiting just *Beyond the Wall.*"

ONCE A-POT A TIME

By Esmeralda Castelan

My poem is a corrido,

as in "Hoy corri yo."

As in

today I have run from a place I once called home and

all that's left is this

dried up stone

of a pot

and here are stained

Mamas fingerprints

and brush strokes

behind them lay

the thought of being tied

behind her back watching her work.

Twinkle in her eye

bright smile

on her face

remembering

how she told me to become better

than her.

But to mankind

I have a

distinct face

I am of a forbidden race

an alien per se

maybe even illegal in a way.

The day I came from my

poor mother's unmentionables

was not there to determine

nor was I destined

to meet the four founding fathers.

My home was obligatory,

standary

but I was ok because

I came from the land where

green avocados made mouths water

where red chili's

made sense tingle

and gringos flee.

Inside me come from that land

the eagle that forsaken

Satans slither.

But corruption must have been dead at hand.

Death and insanitation,

Under the minimum

of minimum wages

Doughy corn and crystallized salt for breakfast

were no strangers

to a lonely man.

A man not full developed

testosterone not yet in full effect.

But what other choice did HE

You

I

We

have

but to pack up your woven colorful flesh on my shoulders

and pocket the 390 pesos

I was thankful to call my own,

and leave.

Having gods tears soak my back

while the earths wet hands

became my platform.

Remembering teachers rant on about the freedom we had gained

to now know that whatever freedom I once had

would soon mean as much

as well,

Trumps heart at the sound of an immigrants' plea.

that I had no place

in the land that was made for

you and me.

But I can still look back in history

and see the battles fought by commoners

and priests.

I can blame Hidalgo from freeing me of "s" with lisps

or light skins with words and actions

as sleek as whips.

Or how Sunday mornings

were committed to my leading lady,

though she may not speak to the basic ear

her songs and grace were meant for our hearts to hear.

Other than God our Virgin Mary is our savior

and

my blood, sweat, and tears

well they come from her.

I give everything to her plus more with golden shrines

and abodes that outshine

my very own home.

I-I just can't cope much longer

and dear lady

I hope that

I did my part.

So, for my years of great service

I let you lay

in broad stripes

and

crisp stars as long as you bless my way.

Once I cross that line

there is no going back.

Once I say goodbye I will no longer be enabled to return to this place.

Though I found my way

becoming your modern-day slave.

Nothing more than

your dirty

tan outlier,

your contracted replaceable space,

puppet on strings

being controlled by your migrating threats.

And why is it that the American dream

only exists for those who can stitch up the seams

in the way that you please?

I no longer fear the

weapons at hand

or the power of man.

My mind is no longer set on the fact that

my skin become your enemy, but my heart here lay as your hidden

friend.

Respect is nowhere near the end.

Respecting the rights of others, what a strange thing I feel,

why does it seem that I'm the only one

this saying adheres to?

My lungs still inhale the same air that yours do.

My lips still quiver, my hands still shake at the same fears, that yours do.

So, if you believe in prayer,

I ask that you pray for us now.

Not just for these tears or for you,

or the black kids jumping double-dutch

the white kid trying weed

or for the man who wears the colorful spectrum

hidden underneath his sleeve,

or for those who feed on his fears.

But for all of us.

Who only have

Mamas fingerprints and brushstrokes

to rely on.

###

ACKNOWLEDGMENTS

Thank you to my parents for constantly pushing me to do astounding things and reminding me that only you choose to add that little "extra" to ordinary. There is nothing on this world that could ever repay everything you've done for me. To Jacqueline for not only helping this dream come to life, but for showing me there is always something more amazing to be done. To all the Chefs, for entrusting an 18-year-old curly haired soñadora with the composition that is you. It's been an honor to share these treasures with the world. To all my friends who never failed to double as my therapists and cheerleaders, you reminded me of my purpose when I thought I had none- YKJKJ. To people like you, who saw something special enough to flip through pages of hope, now go pass it on. And lastly, thank you to the nights that turned into mornings, and my bedroom walls whom have witnessed every headache, tear, and smile throughout this journey your silence became my refuge, and in it I found a little piece of myself. oh! And my dogs :)

— Esmeralda Castelan

Special Thanks to:

JANET LOPEZ
ERICKA LOPEZ
MARIBEL PEREZ
OSCAR FRAGOSO

AND TO EVERYONE ELSE WHO
SUPPORTED ME ON THIS JOURNEY, YOUR
CONTRIBUTIONS MEAN THE WORLD.

www.ingramcontent.com/pod-product-compliance
Lightning Source LLC
Chambersburg PA
CBHW060046100426
42742CB00014B/2711